THRIVING

IN THE

CUSTOMER

AGE

PRAISE FOR THRIVING IN THE CUSTOMER AGE

Today's retail market is evolving from old style store front retail to a fast-paced accelerated retail. Steve has done a masterful job at showing organizations the road map for success in the next decade and beyond. Organizations looking to get to the next level or boost their organizations should embrace this philosophy.

-Jim Kelley, Speaker, Executive Coach, Former Dealership Principle, Sales Executive

*In **"Thriving in the Customer Age"**, Steve has attacked the customer journey in the same thoughtful and precise way that got him to the top of more than 40 summits, including Everest. He makes us challenge conventional thought and always puts the customer experience at the center, driving and inspiring us to be better. His Customer Journey Framework is the perfect and smart guide to getting this right. As an executive and in my case a client, Steve is always passionate about getting it right and doing the right thing. Bravo Steve and thank you for this incredible gift.*

-Shannon Havard, VP Sales, Jim Pattison Broadcast Group

It's almost cliche to say that the business environment is changing quickly. What some fail to understand is that the evolution is outpacing the ability of stalwart businesses to keep up.

This book demystifies one of the most important sales and marketing practices that can help you level up, futureproof your business, and lay down a solid foundation for digital transformation. It's a detailed, step-by-step guide to help you map, design, measure and iterate the customer journey in both B2C and B2B organizations.

Not only does it detail the process and methodology, but also shows you how to track and improve performance of every component resulting in improved revenue and profitability. In my opinion, every organization that wants to compete in the modern marketplace needs to understand these concepts.

-Ernest Barbaric, Executive Coach, Digital Marketing Strategist

The North American Trailer Dealers Association has worked with Steve Whittington for 11+ years. Steve has spoke often at our annual events and been the Keynote Speaker, resulting in overwhelmingly positive feedback from our members. **Thriving in the Customer Age** *is another amazing example of Steve›s vast knowledge of management, sales, marketing data, advertising, service recovery, and customer retention. No matter the size of your dealership or organization, you will benefit from his highly detailed breakdown of the customer journey.*

-Jesse Battle, Executive Director North American Trailer
Dealers Association

ISBN 978-0-9950905-5-2

This book was published with the support of Happful.com

To those that go the extra mile for their customers, you know who you are, you are the future hope of business.

ABOUT THE AUTHOR

CURRENTLY, STEVE WHITTINGTON is Executive Vice President for the Flaman Group of Companies, an award-winning organization. He is also Managing Director of a boutique digital agency, Graphic Intuitions. Steve's current board work includes serving as Chair of the Board for Flaman Fitness Canada, a national retailer; Treasurer of the Glenora Child Care Society; and a member of the Marketing Program Advisory Committee for NAIT's JR Shaw School of Business. Previously, Steve was an Investor/Director for a meal prep internet start-up Mealife, and Chair of the Lethbridge Housing Authority, the third largest social housing NGO in Alberta.

Academically, Steve was a sessional instructor of Project Management at Lethbridge College for seven years. Steve holds a Bachelor of Commerce (Honours) degree; he is a Certified Sales Professional (CSP), Project Management Professional (PMP), and Certified Marketing Specialist (CMS).

Outside his professional life, Steve is a leader in the mountains. An avid mountaineer, he has reached the summit of

49 mountains, including Mount Everest in 2013. On many of his climbs, he has been the expedition leader and/or lead climber. Steve believes his leadership in the mountains has a direct application to his successful leadership in his business life.

LinkedIn: http://ca.linkedin.com/in/sbwhittington

Twitter: @sbwhittington

Company websites:

www.flaman.com;
www.flamanfitness.com
www.graphicintuitions.com;

Personal website: www.stevewhittington.com

To continue your CX learning journey sign up for Steve's monthly insights newsletter.

Contents

THRIVING

IN THE

CUSTOMER

AGE

STEVE WHITTINGTON

INTRODUCTION FROM THE AUTHOR

A DECADE AGO, I didn't know what the "customer journey" was. Though I understood process mapping and lean principles, thought leadership based on the buyer journey was just beginning. There was no discussion of entire company customer journey mapping. Social media as a customer platform was in its infancy, and marketing data and big data were still mostly abstract concepts, as opposed to the ubiquitous applications they are today.

In just over ten years, the confluence of big data, social, mobile, and cloud computing has created a new environment in which businesses operate, leading to new ways in which consumers interact with organizations—and an entirely new set of expectations from these new consumers.

Rewind the clock to 2006. I was firmly entrenched in a traditional business as an executive for the largest light industrial trailer manufacturer in Canada (Southland Trailer Corp.). We were the model of a traditional business. Build the product, push the units to the dealer network locations, and the dealer was then responsible to push the product to the customers' driveways.

Old Business Model

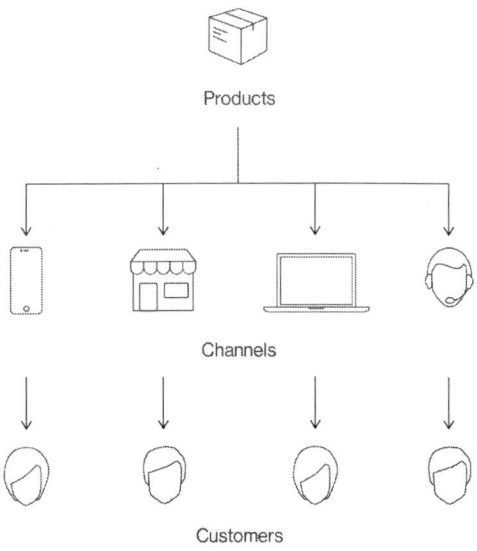

Products

Channels

Customers

Download this graphic and more at stevewhittington.com

Soon, the internet changed everything and, as it is wonderfully described in Tien Tzuo's book, *Subscribed*, a new model emerged. The new model focused on the customer at its center, as opposed to the product. As my career shifted and I moved from production to retail, I experienced first-hand this business model shift and the need to put the customer at the center of the diagram as opposed to the bottom. It was an uncomfortable learning experience.

To help me through this shift and to better understand

it, I consumed volumes of books from thought leaders in digital, analytics, marketing metrics, consumer behaviour, and customer experience; books such as *The Facebook Era, Twitterville, Six Pixels of Separation, Data Driven Marketing, Web Analytics, Conversion, Outside IN, Disney Institute Be Our Guest*, and many others. These books became the body of knowledge that I applied to the businesses I worked with.

To put my new understanding into concrete words, I began blogging in 2010. I started an internal blog called *The Ninth Store* (named for the digital experience at the Flaman Group of Companies, which at the time had eight physical stores; our web presence and emerging e-commerce was "the ninth store"). This blog bridged into weekly internal education sessions in which the knowledge was presented to a broader internal audience. These humble beginnings further bridged into a partnership with a boutique digital agency, Graphic Intuitions, a personal brand website www.stevewhittington. com, speaking, and now this book.

This book takes the hard lessons I learned while struggling through this business transformation and places them in a framework that can be used by any organization to understand, measure, and implement continuous improvement of their most important process: their customer journey.

The book is divided into three sections:

Section One defines the customer journey and the stages of the customer journey. It provides the theoretical base of understanding about the key stages, along with examples and insights highlighting best practices for each stage.

Section Two provides the mathematical framework that is used for continuous customer journey improvement. This section showcases basic metrics and math to holistically measure your customer journey. The importance of each metric is also explained, including what you can learn from each metric and how you can use that knowledge.

Section Three dives into the practical *how*. How do you start to implement the framework to measure your customer journey? If you are not gathering the data required to conduct an analysis, how can you do it? And how do you use this data to train your staff and then create a continuous customer journey improvement loop?

I wrote this book because I believe many organizations and leaders today are grappling with this still-emerging reality. I believe for businesses to "thrive in the customer age" they need to become truly customer-centric. Thus, this book is organized as a workbook with diagrams, worksheets, digestible section summaries and reflections for you to employ as you determine the current management of your customer journey, and to help you determine what you need to do to get where you want to be.

Customer Success means company success. You need a framework to measure your overall customer experience that will provide black and white measurements to guide you. You need to keep score to win in the game of business. This book will teach you how.

-Steve Whittington

WHY FOCUS ON THE
CUSTOMER JOURNEY

IMAGINE BEING PART of a business that had just doubled their top-line revenue in the last four years. Your strategy has been confirmed and you are riding high, confident in your success. Then, over the next two years, sales completely flatline. You are perplexed because the tactics that doubled your revenues were in full swing; in fact, they were being executed with greater effectiveness than in prior years.

As your results stagnated, leads kept pouring into the organization. In fact, leads continued to increase at the same rate they were increasing when the business doubled. Why, then, were sales not continuing to follow?

This was the situation I faced while leading the second largest division of the Flaman Group of Companies. As a member of the executive team, I was baffled. I did not understand.

I felt like we were pouring leads into a bucket with holes in it. Where were the sales? Where were the new customers?

Where were the old customers? In trying to answer these questions as a team, we began to understand that we had been focusing on the wrong data. We knew our top line numbers, our bottom line numbers, our inventory, units moved, turns, and return on investment, but we did not have much data about our customers or about the customer experience. At the time, we could not quantify our customer churn or our true close rate. Nor were we measuring the voice of the customer or segmenting our customers into key accounts, target market profiles, or otherwise.

It wasn't until we viewed our customer experience through a data-based lens that we began to understand. By looking at customer experience data and educating ourselves on customer-centric excellence, we began to learn why our sales had flatlined.

We came to realize that the customer was evolving. The expectations of the customer were changing and, in fact, we as business leaders were beginning to experience the broader customer behavioral shift and the effect it was having on our business. We no longer had a successful formula for revenue growth.

How did this happen?

From television's advent in 1956 to the launch of the Fox TV network in 1986, there were essentially only three television networks in North America, collectively known as the "big three": ABC, CBS, and NBC. These three networks dominated the industry, set expectations for viewers and, for three decades, there was expected stability in the network TV industry, with very little change or disruption. Many similar comparisons can be drawn to the retail landscape during the same time period; the big three in retail, starting with Walmart being founded in 1962 (currently the world's biggest retailer); Kmart (which filed for bankruptcy in 2002 and was acquired by Sears in 2005); and Target. These three dominated the retail landscape for decades. Neither retail consumers nor network viewers had much in terms of choice. **It was the golden age of big brands.**

Fast forward to today, and both industries, like many others, have been completely upended with an almost endless range of options for customers, and competition continues to rise. We all know what changed this paradigm: the internet. In the last 20 years, industries have been in a constant state of white-water; new entrants continue to rise and surpass established leaders. Business models have now changed, and the ways to connect with consumers have also changed. Most importantly, with instant access to information, endless choices, and platforms on which to voice criticisms, consumers have become empowered over brands. The script has been flipped. **We are now in the age of the customer.**

But who is that customer?

Today's customer starts shopping online, wherever they are, at any time. With that 24-hour connectivity, they expect the organizations where they shop to be connected as well. They expect to start the process online and finish in store, or have the process finish through other methods, including delivery, a personal visit, or a follow up call to fulfill their requirements. They expect a seamless, omni-channel experience. They want the experience to be tailored to them, and quickly become disappointed and dismissive when brands do not meet their expectations.

According to the Institute of Customer Service, customer complaints on social media have seen an eight-fold rise since 2014. Initially, the internet educated the consumer, leveling the playing field. With the rise of social media, the consumer was empowered by being given a voice that, for the first time, could significantly hurt brands that mistreated customers. We now see endless examples of consumers lashing out at brands via social media platforms, to the extent that social channels such as Twitter are considered by many communication professionals to be customer support channels, as opposed to simply being promotional branding channels.

With ample education as to available products and services and with globalization providing endless choice, there is also always another organization willing to meet a customer's expectations.

In addition to this customer empowerment, the old way of specialization within organizations for delivering greater efficiencies within traditional Sales, Marketing, Operations, and Customer Service silos, is now creating a disjointed experience. Instead of increasing satisfaction, these silos create frustration and dissatisfaction for the customer.

Consider a typical service interaction, such as a hotel or vehicle rental, or any organization in which you have an account. How many times does a consumer have to repeat their information to spend money or resolve an issue? How is this repetition across organizational silos a good customer experience? This repetition and inefficiency leads to frustration and dissatisfaction, which customers are all too willing to promptly share on social and review platforms!

To mitigate the problems caused by these silos, customer success teams are now being created to manage the customer experience. These teams function as a customer quarterback to help customers quickly obtain their solution, aided by integrated systems and automations to complete tasks, which auto populate a customer's information. This automation is the next step many organizations are taking to create a new normal for meeting customer expectations. It is important to note that in today's connected world, the seamless experience a customer receives in one industry creates a similar expectation for every other industry. As an organization, you are no longer competing solely with peers in your industry; you are competing with a general rising tide of expectations.

For organizations to successfully navigate this disruption, there is only one option: obsessive focus on customers and the customer journey your organization provides. Organizations must map and measure the entire customer journey in order to understand it from the customer's point of view. It is only with this understanding, by measuring all steps in the journey, do brands have an opportunity to improve their customer experience and thus their business results.

The path is clear: **Becoming customer-centric = becoming data-centric; becoming customer-centric = being profit-centric.**

Section One
DEFINING THE CUSTOMER JOURNEY

TODAY, AS I look at the overall retail and service landscape, I see organizations failing to meet customer expectations. The list of storied brands shutting down their physical locations is enormous. In 2017 alone, over 5,000 stores from major retailers were closed: Sears and Kmart closed 358 stores in 2017, only to file for bankruptcy in 2018. Also in 2017, JC Penney closed 138 stores, Macy's closed 68 stores, and Payless Shoes emerged from its Chapter 11 restructuring with almost 1,000 fewer stores, only to shut down entirely in February 2019. In 2018, the list grew to include Lowes shutting down locations, Victoria's Secret closing stores, Mattress Firm shutting down 700 locations, Brookstone closing 102 mall locations and filing for bankruptcy protection, and the list goes on and on.

The reasons for this are many: customers can now educate themselves independent of information most in-store representatives provide. A retail store is limited by the brands they offer, while a customer may want alternatives that are available instantly online. The store itself is inconvenient;

customers must travel to a location on their own time, often off-route. Then, by adding another layer comprised of—at best—average customer service, it is easy to understand why customers are heading to direct-to-brand or e-commerce sites in ever-increasing numbers. These days, e-commerce continues to grow by double digits annually, taking a bigger and bigger bite out of the retail pie.

E-commerce as a channel for service is creating an issue in and of itself for brands. While booking services online is a convenience for the customer, fierce cost comparisons are driving prices down, and customer service training and staffing tend to get cut to keep prices competitive.

In the US, e-commerce accounts for 13% of all retail, and will soon rise to 15%. This trend suggests that brick and mortar retail is doomed, as is any B2B brand whose products can be purchased directly.

If brick and mortar retail is doomed, why would a host of online brands now be opening physical retail stores? Trunk Club, Warby Parker, UNTUCKit, and many more online retailers have done so, along with Amazon purchasing 460 Whole Foods stores. What's going on? Is retail dead? Or is it just bad retail? From the outside, the answer seems clear: online brands have always been obsessively focused on the customer experience, and they realize the best customer experience can still be achieved in person as part of an omni-channel ecosystem. This understanding has allowed them to bring their customer experience mastery into the physical world.

If you are not Amazon or Warby Parker, what's an organization to do?

The highest priority of an organization must be to focus on the customer by creating the best experience for the customer in every interaction. This focus is not a new insight, and should be a simple enough priority. Then why is it not happening consistently? One answer is that brick and mortar retail organizations, unlike online retailers, have not been obsessively mapping every step of the customer journey. Online retailers are now bringing this thinking to traditional retail locations. Traditional retail needs to embrace this obsession with customer-centric thinking if it hopes to survive and thrive.

While this practice is simple for one person (or one website) with the right mindset to understand and execute, most organizations have multiple team members and multiple locations facing the customer. With organizational diversity, doing what is the best for the customer can take on multiple definitions with multiple outcomes. Consistency thus becomes an issue. The only way to create consistency is to map the customer journey and define the desired customer outcome for each touchpoint. Each of these touchpoints should be viewed as "a moment of truth" for meeting the desired customer expectation.

The challenge for brands is to train their teams holistically about the full customer journey, within a framework that can be used to measure and subsequently improve the customer journey, much like the analytics used for website optimization.

This measurement framework will be covered in Section Two. However, let's begin by answering a simple question:

WHAT IS THE CUSTOMER JOURNEY?

A broad definition of the customer journey is this: **all the interactions or touchpoints a customer has with an organization previous, during and after the purchase and/or service experience**. These interactions start with the first awareness of a need for a product or service, and continue through the completion of the transaction and after-service elements.

While this journey is often portrayed as linear (and it certainly can be with transactional customers), with relationship customers, the journey can be a continuous loop—as opposed to a linear path. The journey can actually be broken into four distinct stages: 1) Awareness/Consideration, 2) Sale Process, 3) After Sale Process, and 4) Retention and Referral.

Download this graphic and more at stevewhittington.com

Drawing the focus of every member of an organization's team to the customer journey is the single-most important thing a company can do.

Understanding the four stages of the customer journey is the first step for any organization to providing a consistent customer experience. Once the stages are understood, an organization can embark on mapping their customer journey to create a baseline against which improvements can be measured.

Stage 1
AWARENESS/CONSIDERATION

AT SOME POINT in time, your customer had identified a need for your product or service. Somehow, your customer learned about your organization and decided to connect. Understanding your customer's connection with your organization (how did they become aware of your product or service?) and the outcome of that connection (conversion into a lead) is the first step in evaluating the effectiveness of your customer journey. The initial connection might arise from advertising, a web search, reviews, store signage, referral from a current customer, product labeling, or other sources. This is Stage 1, and the impression all these touchpoints make will influence whether a customer converts into a lead, then a sales opportunity or, more importantly, a customer relationship opportunity.

Stage 1 may appear to simply describe marketing and advertising; for the most part, that's true, but it goes deeper. Marketing and advertising require the proper intent to initiate a truly positive customer journey instead of intrusive awareness, which is not a good start to a customer journey.

Let me explain. Most ads showcase a product and an offer, and ideally are targeted appropriately. The creative element is prepared within branding guidelines. The job of any ad is to have an attractive enough offer to entice the customer to act.

Causing the customer to act creates a lead for the sale process to take over. On to Stage 2.

But wait. What if your ad did more than merely provide an offer? What if your ad solved a problem or connected with a customer's interest? The Awareness/Consideration stage is the start of the customer journey, and thus provides the first filter for how a brand's customer journey will be perceived. If you broadcast only offers, your message is transactional. If you broadcast messages that solve problems for your customers or connect with their interests, the message is that you "get" your customers. The *intent* of your awareness tactics sets the tone for Stage 2.

INSIGHT

THE IMPACT OF GOOD AND BAD ADVERTISING

There is good advertising, and there is bad advertising. Some advertising creates powerful emotional responses, and some advertising is so vacuous that it creates basically no impression at all. Considering the typical response rate, I would argue that most advertising is vacuous in nature, and is in fact **a tax brands pay for not taking care of their customers**.

But what difference does good advertising or bad advertising make? Starting at the Awareness/Consideration stage, what is the impact of advertising and promotion on the entire customer journey?

Let's look at a bad example first: Dove's diversity of beauty ad.

Dove "Body wash – Diversity of Beauty"

Dove's intent with this ad was to show the depth of the diversity of beauty, but it read to many observers as anti-black and ended up being tagged as a top Google search result for "Dove Racist Ad." This, in turn, created a PR nightmare for the firm. There is no way that this ad created a positive impact at the start of the customer journey. In fact, through this ad, Dove created an ethical barrier for their brand that customers now need to hurdle in order to choose their products. A customer may consider that buying Dove products conveys support for an organization that just doesn't care about race issues. That is a stance no consumer wants to take.

The impact of this 3-second Gif was such that is was posted Friday and taken down Saturday, and received negative media coverage worldwide. Dove promptly issued the following apology:

> "This [ad] did not represent the diversity of real beauty which is something Dove is passionate about and is core to our beliefs, and it should not have happened. We apologize deeply and sincerely for the offense that it has caused and do not condone any activity or imagery that insults any audience."

This ad did not provide a good start for the Dove customer journey.

Contrast this ad with P&G's "Thank You, Mom" ad. This ad campaign currently consists of three spots, which started with the 2012 London Olympics ("Best Job"), the 2014 Sochi Olympics ("Pick Them Back Up"), the 2016 RIO Olympics ("Strong"), and is slated to continue into 2020 as it still resonates with consumers. It is a feel-good story that was created to support the P&G branding initiative of sponsoring the Olympic Games.

P&G "Thank you Mom"

All the ads focus on the journey a mother takes with her daughter or son athlete, from teaching them to walk, to teaching them the sport they become an athlete in, to being supportive through it all. The intent of the ad is to make a connection with mothers around the world who are supportive of their children. With this ad, P&G is saying to mothers that "we get you" and "we are here to support you." Empathy, understanding, and support. P&G is making customers aware of their brands by using a common place of connection.

A great place for the start of the P&G customer journey.

The intent communicated by a brand's Awareness/Consideration activities sets the stage for the rest of the customer journey.

For a brand to effectively set the tone in the Awareness/Consideration stage, the importance of a consistent, clear brand voice tied to organizational values has never been more important.

An off-brand ad (not using your brand voice) can be devastating to an organization. When an ad is viewed, it *becomes* the organization in the customer's perception.

The Awareness/Consideration stage extends to all promotional activities, especially in social media. The impact of a poorly worded tweet can be just as bad or good as a multi-million dollar 30-second TV spot. Brands that seek to solve their customer problems by dispensing expert advice or connecting to their customer with empathy, as opposed to yell-and-sell offers, will align with their customer needs and thus create higher engagement and an ultimately higher conversion rate.

With modern customer tracking, marketers can learn how many nurturing touches are required before a potential customer commits to a conversion activity such as requesting information or requesting a quote. Truly integrated campaigns across traditional, social, and owned channels can be measured and continuously improved upon.

Stage 1
SUMMARY AND REFLECTIONS

SUMMARY

The Awareness/Consideration phase includes every medium a brand uses to message the customer.

- These mediums go beyond traditional out-bound and digital media.

- They include the experience created by your business development team and the impression your business makes in the world.

The intent of all your promotional activities sets the tone for the subsequent stages, and ultimately affects your conversion rate from these activities.

A classic example of setting the tone is the all-too-often used discount offer, which is combined with scarcity close tactics on traditional channels:

"Our furniture blowout is this weekend only. Couches start at $499 for a limited time, don't miss

out on this amazing deal! The other stores don't know how we can go this low! At these prices we won't be able to keep stock for long, so come on down today!"

The only value being credited is the discount that is being offered (if it is indeed a very competitive discount). There is no relationship being created. The customer will only buy if the offer is enticing enough to create the motivation for a transactional purchase.

Compare the above discount offer with the following message:

"Deciding how to decorate your home can be a daunting task, we have been helping customers design efficient and stylish living spaces for 20 years, and we want to help you. Use our free interior lay-out tool online or drop by one of our 5 locations for a free interior design consultation. Let us help you create the living space you desire."

The intent of this ad is to consult with the customer and help them realize the living space of their dreams. The offer is based on building a relationship, not a one-time transaction.

The intent of your ad sets the tone for start of your customer journey.

REFLECTIONS

- What is your brand voice?
- How would you describe the intent of your organization's promotional activities?

- Are you being transactional or relationship building?
- Are you being a trusted advisor, biggest fan, or interrupter of customer activities with the message you are conveying?

Stage 2
THE SALE PROCESS

THE FIRST "SALES" touch a customer receives about your organization is most likely not something you created. Your marketing may have created an itch, and due to the digitization of our world, it drove the customer to the internet.

According to a study conducted by marketing intelligence agency Mintel, **70% of consumers read reviews before purchasing, with 90% of consumers reporting that reviews impacted their buying decision.** In other words, the experiences posted online by previous buyers are influencing your future buyers. This fact alone is a compelling reason to make a positive customer experience your number one priority!

If you pass the internet and social media word-of-mouth test, the next place a consumer is likely to land is your website. There, the customer should be able to easily find product/service information and the ability to be educated to make a purchase in the way they desire. For e-commerce, B2C brands, or a more complex B2B service, the customer needs to clearly know what the next step is for them in their customer journey, and must have all the information required to be comfortable in making that decision. If the website only serves as a lead funnel to drive consumers to brick and mortar locations, it's simply serving the brand and not the customer. In this case, you stand a very good chance of driving the customer to another website instead of to your location.

But if the website can get the customer interested in your product or service, is informative, and helps them in their buyer's journey, they will then contact you—and they have now been converted into a lead. When this happens, you must have a process in place that ensures a consistent customer experience for handling of incoming leads across all channels, one that can be monitored and improved upon. If this process is mismanaged, you will not get the customer to your location, nor will you capture the customer information required to be able to nurture this lead. In response to the multi-channel world that brands and consumers are immersed in, customer success teams that can manage all incoming channels to create a consistent voice have emerged. In some organizations, all web forms, chat conversations, emails, and initial phone calls are being managed by the same team, creating a consistent process and voice for the organization to engage with the customer.

Consider that a customer success team does not need to consist of full-time dedicated resources. Your organization could be a small team, ranging from 3–15 people in total, and yet still have a customer success team. Whoever manages the incoming leads across various channels can be brought together to form a customer success team by using a consistent process that is trackable, and thus able to be monitored for improvement. This "team" could be as simple as a receptionist/admin resource that handles the first touch phone calls and walk-ins, plus monitors the company's social and web forms, combined with two inside sales people and a service technician. In this case, being a member of the customer success team is not a full-time job, but rather is a united purpose. The team is formed to create a consistent process for the customer by individuals in an organization that would otherwise not be united on this process due to their full-time job functions, which may pull them in different directions.

BEST PRACTICE

THE FOUR STEPS TO FOLLOW FOR A PHONE LEAD

Imagine you work for an organization that sells industrial equipment. Your buyers are generally not shoppers, but customers that have a product solution need: they need to haul a skid steer to the job site, and they need a flatdeck trailer to move it. This is not a want but a need. Many organizations exhibit this buying behavior. In today's digital world, the phone call is often the first human-to-human contact, and as such is very important. Yet, all too often, the incoming call is mishandled as follows:

Sales Person: "Sales, how can I help you?"

Customer: "I'm looking for product Z. What do you have?"

Sales Person: "We have it in this color with these options in stock."

Customer: "What's the price?"

Sales Person "We have that one for $XX,995"

Customer: "Hmmm, I will think about it."

Sales Person: "OK, perfect, thanks for calling. If you need anything else, call back and ask for Greg."

While the above transcript is an abridged version of an incoming sales call, the framework is unfortunately all too true for lead management in many retail organizations.

So, what's wrong with this call? The customer called in, they requested information and were provided the answer. This is good customer service, right? Actually, it is not. It ultimately does not serve the customer, nor the organization. Here's why:

- Marketing creates attention to cause incoming leads.

- The job of the sales team is to convert the leads to sales.

- The above handling of an incoming lead does not convert the lead to a sales opportunity.

Rather, the steps to follow with an incoming phone lead are simple:

- **Capture the lead**
- **Qualify the lead**
- **Advance the sale**
- **Set the next action**

Sadly, in many organizations these steps do not occur with consistency. The outcomes of following this simple four-step process can be transformative. Sales can double, and an organization's customer service will increase significantly due to the professional process of the sales team.

Let's further define these steps, by reviewing the old way, and then considering a more effective approach.

CAPTURE THE LEAD

Objective: In this step, the focus of the salesperson is to capture the customer information to create a lead. Without the customer contact information, the phone call is just a social conversation with the hope that the customer will follow up to become a true lead. Hope is not a business strategy.

Old Way: Not capturing the lead

Sales Person: "Sales, how can I help you?"

Customer: "I'm looking for product Z. What do you have?"

Sales Person: "We have this in this color with these options in stock."

New Way: Capturing the lead

Sales Person: "Sales, how can I help you?"

Customer: "I'm looking for product Z. What do you have?"

Sales Person: "Sir, just in case this call gets dropped can I get your name and phone number so I can call you back immediately."

Customer: "Sure, I'm Bob Johnston at 612.345.4455."

Sales Person: "Thanks, Bob. My name is Greg Smith. Nice to meet you. So you are looking for product Z...."

While this will not work 100% of the time, you will be surprised at how often it does work, due to the amount of mobile phone usage. The ask accomplishes two things: 1) it captures the lead, and 2) lets the customer know you are serious about customer service, as you want to ensure that if anything happens during the call you can re-establish contact immediately to continue helping them.

Now the salesperson has a lead. Without getting the customer name and contact information there is no lead.

Sales Tip: Having the customer's name at the start

of the process allows the salesperson to build rapport faster, by immediately using the customer's name.

QUALIFY THE LEAD

Objective: In this step there are two tasks: qualifying the product or service need and qualifying the buying intent.

First, the salesperson uses their product knowledge to work with the customer to determine the best product offering that would meet their specific need.

Second, while doing this, the salesperson needs to prompt for or listen for buying signals that will indicate the customer's purchasing timeline. The customer can be buying today, next week, next month, or six months from now; it is the salesperson's job to figure out how hot this prospect is.

Old way: Not qualifying the lead

Customer: "I'm looking for product Z. What do you have?"

Sales Person: "We have it in this color with these options in stock."

Customer: "What's the price?"

Sales Person "We have one for $XX,995."

New way: Qualifying the lead

Customer: "I'm looking for product Z. What do you have?"

Sales Person: "Sir, just in case this call gets dropped can I get your name and phone number so I can call you back immediately."

Customer: "Sure, I'm Bob Johnston at 612.345.4455."

Sales Person: "Thanks, Bob. My name is Greg Smith. Nice to meet you. So, you are looking for product Z. Well, Bob, do you mind if I ask you a few questions (*this is where your product and industry knowledge come into play, such as what you need to do with product Z, and the frequency of use*)? This will help me determine what the best product solution for your need is."

Customer: "Well, I am looking at moving X once or twice a month."

Sales person: "OK, thanks Bob. So you need to do this (moving X), but not often. Do you have a budget in mind?"

Customer: "Yeah, since I am not going to use it much, I just need something as cost effective as possible to do the job when needed."

Sales Person: "Got it. And when do you need this by, Bob?"

Customer: "Next week."

Now, the salesperson has qualified the customer product or service requirement and qualified the lead as a hot one that needs immediate attention. There is also a clear buying signal: "Next week."

When compared to the old way, when a salesperson simply answers the question asked of them, the salesperson may be misquoting the customer, as they have not qualified the customer's need. The customer may think they know all the options, but the salesperson is the expert on this product and as such it is the salesperson's job to help the customer understand the best options for their need. The risk is that the customer will next call a competitor and ask for product Z and be quoted a lower price without any qualification. The customer simply thinks company B has a lower cost, and they will go with that company; the salesperson never receives a call back. Another issue is that the old way provides no indication of time sensitivity. In the new way, the salesperson knows Bob needs this product next week.

Sales Tip: Qualifying the above conversation could have easily gone the other way, in which the customer has a need of high use, and thus requires a higher quality product to stand up to commercial applications—the price may not be the deciding factor. Determining the customer's need helps with understanding the price sensitivity and thereby anticipating the customer's objections.

ADVANCE THE SALE

Objective: In this step, the salesperson has one requirement: move the sale toward a buyer commitment.

Old way: Just answer questions

> Customer: "What's the price?"
>
> Sales Person "We have one for $XX,995."
>
> Customer: "Hmmm, I will think about it."

New way: Creating buyer commitment

> Customer: "Next week."
>
> Sales Person: "Well, Bob, based upon what we have discussed, we have a number of options in stock ready for next week. The range in price is XXXX to XXXX (from high to low). Can we set a time for you to come in to review the products?"
>
> Customer: "Sure, I will come by today."

There are many ways this conversation may have gone. The customer may not want to come in, or they may be looking for a custom quote. In that case, the salesperson needs to advance the sale by making a commitment to the customer.

Alternate way:

> Sales Person: "Well, Bob, based upon what we have discussed, we have a number of options in stock ready

for next week. The range in price is XXXX to XXXX (from high to low). Can we set a time for you to come in to review the products?"

Customer: "No. I am still just gathering information right now."

Sales Person: "I understand, Bob. Can I send you some product literature and a quote to help you with your process?"

Customer: "Yes, that would work."

While the salesperson has not gotten the customer into the retail location, they have still advanced the sale process.

Sales Tip: There is always a way to advance the sale, whether through setting an appointment, sending information, or acquiring an email for newsletter sign up. The key is to get the customer to commit to another action. This continues to build the customer relationship and provides service toward meeting the customer's need.

SET THE NEXT ACTION

Objective: Never lose control of the sale process by using a weak ending. Even without a clear buyer commitment, you should maintain control of the sale process by setting the next action, and thus planting an expectation in the customer's mind.

Old way: Not setting the next action

Customer: "Hmmm, I will think about it."

Sales Person: "OK, perfect, thanks for calling. If you need anything else, call back and ask for Greg."

New way: Setting the next action

Customer: "Sure, I will come by today."

Sales Person: "This morning or afternoon? I want to make sure I have everything ready for you."

Customer: "This afternoon."

Sales Person: "Thanks, Bob. I appreciate you taking the time to call. I will expect to see you this afternoon. If I do not see you by 3:30, I will give you a call to confirm. Does that work for you?"

Customer: "Yes, it does. I will see you then."

Sales Person: "Thanks for your call, Bob. I will have the product ready for you this afternoon."

Sales Tip: Most people will honour their commitments. If the customer has committed to coming in and viewing the product, they will likely show up. Now the salesperson has an opportunity to wow the customer with an amazing customer experience and a display of product knowledge. If the customer has objections, the salesperson can deal with them face to face. Finally, being grateful and polite is free, so always thank the customer for the opportunity.

Alternate way

Sales Person: "I understand, Bob. Can I send you some product literature and a quote to help you with your process?"

Customer: "Yes, that would work."

Sales Person: "Can I get your email address so I can send you files? I can also drop a brochure in the mail."

Customer: "My email is bobjohnston1@gmail.com, and my mailing address is ...."

Sales Person: "I will get the quote emailed to you today and drop a brochure in the mail. I will give you a couple of days to review, and then I am going to call you on Thursday to see if you have any questions."

Customer: "Thursday will not work."

Sales Person: "No problem. Can I call you Friday morning?"

Customer: "That will work."

Sales Person: "OK, I will call you Friday at 9:00 am at 612.345.4455 to review the quote. I will also have a list of products we have in stock that we can review. Does this work for you?"

Customer: "Yes."

Sales Person: "Bob, thanks for calling in. I will send this information to you today and am looking forward to reviewing any questions Friday. Talk to you then."

CONCLUSION

While no process is flawless, and individual personalities will shine through, consistently following this four-step process will increase the effective management of incoming phone sales leads and spike close rates. Note that although this process was outlined for use on a phone call, the exact same process can be used for chat engines. Web forms will follow a marketing automation process that will "warm a lead up" to get the consumer to an agent interaction. Once the agent interaction occurs, the same process follows.

The point is to create consistency throughout the process and measure the outcomes towards your goal.

If the phone call goes well, the customer is going to come to the store. Every touchpoint is going to influence their buying decision. The sign, the parking lot, entrance, showroom, retail floor or lobby, the initial greeting: all these touchpoints set the tone before your customer-facing staff has a chance to engage with the customer.

Now, once the customer begins to engage with a member of your front-line staff, their product knowledge, company attire, selling space, and use of a clear frictionless process influences the customer, helping them to decide whether or not to make a purchase.

You may be thinking, "How does staff attire affect the tone of the buying environment?" The culmination of details matter! If a location is messy and the staff are not friendly or easy to recognize (wearing street attire instead of branded company attire), all these touchpoints add up to create an experience for the customer. With the above example, the tone or feel of the store experience being created could be "We don't care." When a customer "feels" like the brand doesn't care, how likely are they to make a buying decision? Add to the above environment, perhaps the store is short staffed that day and there is a long wait for the customer to be helped. The lack of staff adds friction (increasing wait time) to a process that creates no customer value, detracting from the chance of the customer making a purchase.

Now, suppose the customer makes the decision to purchase, they have now committed to your brand. Or have they? The next two stages will turn this customer into one that promotes, is neutral, or is a detractor who writes negative reviews.

Stage 2
SUMMARY AND REFLECTIONS

SUMMARY

UNDERSTAND THAT ONCE the customer is interested in your brand, they will conduct research. The outcomes of previous customer experiences with your brand are now going to influence this new customer's buying decision. Reputation management is a key metric that will be discussed in later sections, by explaining the process and how to gather positive reviews.

The Sale Process ensures that all your customer acquisition paths have clearly defined steps that can be measured and improved upon. Section Two will dive deeper into the measurement of these steps.

Whether this is a returning customer or new customer, the start of a new journey is the same, and can follow the same four steps:

1. Capture the Lead

2. Qualify the Lead

3. Advance the Sale

4. Set the Next Action

REFLECTIONS

- Do you have a sale process in place that is documented for all of your sales team to follow? Is it being measured?

- Think about what you can do to measure your sale process, and then use the results to teach and improve your team.

- How many leads do you think your organization receives that are not captured?

- What is your close rate?

Stage 3
THE AFTER SALE PROCESS

EVERY ORGANIZATION HAS an after sale process; the question is to determine how well it is managed for the customer. For some organizations, it is product training and delivery; for other businesses (restaurants or hotels), service is provided after the purchase decision. No matter the organization, there are many touchpoints after the sale. It is often the last touchpoint that the customer remembers, and this is the one that can define how a customer "feels" about an organization.

The last touchpoint a customer has with an organization can make or break their entire customer journey.

Consider a typical retail experience, in which a customer buys a piece of furniture and needs to pick up the unit at the loading doors around the back of the store. Throughout the process during the front of store experience everything was great; the organization's staff were friendly, informative, and genuinely helpful. The customer left the front of the store feeling great. When they arrived at the back, however, the attendee was rude, unfriendly, and made them wait long enough that they suspected that they had been forgotten. Finally, when the furniture arrived, the box was damaged. They mentioned this to the attendee and were told to take it or leave it.

How do you suppose the customer now feels about this entire customer journey?

Flip this story around: the front of store interactions were mediocre at best, but there was a good price, so the customer bought, then went to the back of the store and the service was amazing. How do you suppose the customer feels about this entire customer journey?

The point is that exceptional service is not the result of exceptional experiences; it results from carefully designed processes that are executed flawlessly. An exceptional customer experience is not beyond any organization. Exceptional service can be designed into systems organizational leaders control, and is about creating an entire system of processes that have measurable standards and a recovery process for when things go wrong. (Things will go wrong; they always do, and how you respond to them is more important than how you behave when things go right.)

Exceptional service that creates an exceptional experience comes down to four areas:

1. The careful design of the customer journey.

2. The intentional flawless delivery of the customer experience (every touchpoint matters, every touchpoint is a moment of truth before and after the sale).

3. The measurement of the system for learning and improvement.

4. Construction of a recovery system for when things do not go according to plan.

BEST PRACTICE

WHAT MAKES FOR A GOOD RECOVERY SYSTEM?

A good system starts with the acknowledgment that organizations are made of people, and that people are not perfect. Therefore, mistakes will happen. How an organization deals with a mistake is often more important than the mistake itself.

Generally, mistakes are because one of two things happened:

1. Something that was expected to happen did not happen.

2. Someone did not communicate to a customer about what is happening.

Both are functions of customer expectations and the emotions that come with failure to meet those expectations. The customer expects something to have occurred, or the customer expects timely (as defined by the customer) communication about what is or isn't occurring.

When expectations are not met, a simple five-step recovery system can be followed:

1. Take ownership
2. Listen
3. Empathise
4. Apologize
5. Refocus towards a solution

Using this system, let's look at a real-world example. Your customer was expecting that a unit would be ready to be picked up and it has not arrived. The customer needs this unit for their job site, and the unit's unavailability is impairing their ability to do their job. Using the recovery system, what do you do?

I am sure we have all experienced this situation at some point in our life. We ordered something either in the B2C space or B2B space, and it did not arrive when promised. Most times, I am told there is nothing the organization can do, and that it is not their fault, but their supplier's fault. Actually, it is their fault, and if this happens to your customers, it is your fault as well.

Step 1: Take Ownership

No matter what has happened to your customer, you need to take 100% responsibility for their experience.

Whether a supplier delivery is late, or it is the result of another departments' actions or inactions, by owning the customer experience with 100% responsibility you show you care.

For the sake of illustration, each step will have a role play included that highlights a typical customer experience with a no recovery system and how a customer experience goes with a recovery system.

> Customer: "My X is late. What are you going to do about it? It was supposed to be here today! I need it today."

> Staff with No Recovery System: "I'm sorry. The carrier has not shown up yet. Could you check back in an hour? It should be here by then."

> Staff with Recovery System: "Let me look into this right away. Can I get your details so I can start to track the package? I am going to work on finding this package for you, so you have it today."

Step 2: Listen

Listening also shows you care. Your customer is frustrated because whatever they expected to happen did not happen. You need to hear them and understand why they are upset. Learn how their unmet expectations affect them.

> Customer: "It was supposed to be here today! I need it today."

> Staff with No Recovery System: "Please check back in an hour. Hopefully it will have arrived by then."
>
> Staff with Recovery System: "I am going to work on finding this package for you, so you have it today. What do you need X for today?"
>
> Customer: "I need it at my job site. Without it the job will be held up."

Now you know the level of importance, because you cared enough to ask a question seeking to understand. This action allows for Step 3 to occur.

Step 3: Empathize

Your customer's frustration is completely understandable. Tell your customer that they have every right to be upset. This is going to affect their ability to do X.

> Customer: "I need it at my job site. Without it, the job will be held up."
>
> Staff with No Recovery System: "I'm sorry. I wish there was something I could do."
>
> Staff with Recovery System: "You have every right to be upset. This could affect your livelihood. I would be upset, too."

Step 4: Apologize

At this point, you have taken responsibility for the unmet expectation, listened to your customer's grievances, and empathized with them. Now, it is time for a sincere apology; that is sometimes all a customer is looking for, but you are going to do more.

> Customer: "I need it at my job site. Without it, the job will be held up."
>
> Staff with No Recovery System: "I'm sorry. I wish there was something I could do."

Note this is the same as the Step 3 response for the Staff with No Recovery System for customer-facing staff. They have no options. They can only apologize, an apology that, despite their level of sincerity, will leave the customer feeling incomplete and dissatisfied.

> Staff with Recovery System: "You have every right to be upset. This could affect your livelihood. I would be upset, too. I take full responsibility. The experience you are having is not how our organization wants anyone to feel. This is not acceptable, and I sincerely apologize."

Step 5: Refocus toward a solution

After the apology, it is now time to resolve the issue by diagnosing the problem. Customers do not need to hear why the problem occurred; that doesn't help them. It is time for you to tell your customer what you are going to do about their issue. This may be as simple as letting them know that you are going to immediately go to your manager and get back to them within 30 minutes, or maybe there is a ready solution available. Either way, the last step moves toward a solution for your customer and ends the conversation with the customer feeling that something is being done on their behalf.

Staff with No Recovery System: This customer-facing staff has no options, so the exchange ended with an apology that offered no solution.

> Staff with Recovery System: "This is not acceptable, and I sincerely apologize. Now, this is what I am going to do to resolve this issue. Our organization can do _____."

Customers are people. When something goes wrong, they want acknowledgment and a solution. It is quite simple if tools and training are provided to your customer-facing staff. Depending on your business, you may have to get creative, but if you work at it you will find that most of your issues can be resolved by providing a few options for your staff to call upon. Better yet, after the issue occurs, create a process to ensure that it never occurs again.

According to Esteban Kolsky (from research for an annual customer experience statistics list), if customers are not satisfied, **13% of them will tell 15 or more people that they are unhappy.** On the other hand, **72% of customers will share a positive experience with 6 or more people**.

Every touchpoint matters. The impact of the execution of all the touchpoints in first three stages of
the customer journey can be measured by using the
Net Promoter System (one of the KPIs described and
defined in Section Two), which asks one simple question: how likely are you to recommend? This leads us
to Stage 4.

Always keep in mind that the last touchpoint will define
how you make your customer feel about the entire customer journey. Your customer will not remember the great
price and helpful staff at the start of their journey; they will
remember the last touchpoint and how it made them feel.
**And how your organization made them feel will be what
they share both as word-of-mouth and online.**

Stage 3
SUMMARY AND REFLECTIONS

SUMMARY

MANY ORGANIZATIONS DISPLAY a tremendous amount of focus, right to the point of the transaction. Often what happens next is delivered by staff with high turnover and small amounts of training. All the effort that went into capturing the lead and getting the customer to commit can be wiped clean by a poor after sale process. As much care and attention as goes into the front half of the journey needs to be put into the back half.

Exceptional service is a system. Take the time to create yours in such a way that it can be easily trained, measured and thus improved upon.

REFLECTIONS

- What is your after sale process? Is there a checklist that can be followed and provided to the customer

as quality control for this stage? Think PDI (Pre-Delivery Inspection) for automobiles.

- Do you have a recovery system, and are all your customer-facing staff trained and empowered? Many leaders default to, "Yes, my staff is empowered." Ask your staff or conduct a survey to find out what your staff really think they are supposed to do or allowed to do. Some staff think they are doing the right thing by denying warranty claims, for example, because warranty claims can cost the company money and denying claims saves the company money. It might in the short term, but losing a customer may be far costlier than a claim.

Stage 4
RETENTION AND REFERRAL

ASSUMING THAT YOUR customer journey has created a positive experience, you may be turning customers into promoters that feed new people into Stage 1: Awareness/ Consideration to start a journey with your organization.

The ongoing experience with an organization will help or detract from customer retention and referral. Every time your customer uses your product or remembers the experience they had with your services, good will, neutral will, or bad will is built. If a warranty issue is handled poorly, the good will goes down. Alternately, if the warranty issue is handled fairly and promptly, the good will can go up. The point of this stage is to retain customers, turn them into promoters, and stop them from leaving (customer churn).

Research suggests that the reasons customers are not retained are not often reported to the organization. Referring again to Esteban Kolsky's *50 Customer Experience Statistics* derived from his annual survey:

- **67% of customers mention bad experiences as a**

> **reason for leaving an organization or not repurchasing, but only 1 out of 26 unhappy customers complain.**
>
> • **66% of consumers who switched brands did so because of poor service.**

As alarming as these statistics are, companies that pay attention to their customer care process and exhibit the consideration to reach out and really work to retain their customers should be hopeful. From the same survey, in the context of customer care and consideration (or lack thereof), consider the following statistics:

> • **85% of customer churn due to poor service is preventable.**
>
> • **11% of customer churn could be prevented by simple company outreach.**
>
> • **67% of customer churn is preventable if the customer issue is resolved at the first engagement.**

Wow! Companies that care about more than just a sale have a good chance to keep a customer for the long-term.

So how does a brand do this? Reaching out to gather feedback about your customers' experiences is one touchpoint showing them the company cares. Ongoing touches matter, as well. This stage of retention and referral demands a simple process in which the company contacts the customer to ensure that everything went well with a purchase experience, and then uses the recovery system from Stage 3 to immediately resolve any issues. Moreover, in a B2B environment or subscription revenue model, retention and referral is an essential part of strategic account management. An organization using strategic account management actively works towards becoming a trusted advisor with key accounts. This position is accomplished by providing solutions to help the business they serve improve. Truly, organizations using strategic account management understand that customer success equals their success. As such, the intent of ongoing follow up is to help determine the next step a customer can take to reach their business goals.

This process isn't limited to B2B accounts. B2C brands that sell any kind of good or service can also benefit from the same kind of follow up in support of an ongoing relationship. For instance, imagine an outdoor retailer that sells a slackline (high tension line used for fun, improving balance and core strength). After the purchase, why wouldn't a customer enjoy an email about how to get started and improve their technique? Beyond that, why wouldn't the customer enjoy an ongoing touch to see how things are going, with additional intermediate tips, plus the suggestion to consider a wobble board for enhanced training? This is classic marketing automation using a drip nurturing campaign. Engaging this process post purchase flips the before-sale script to keep the customer loyal for the next sale.

The technology for this type of automation is available, and the techniques are known; brands need to merely shift their efforts and intention.

BEST PRACTICE

STRATEGIC ACCOUNT MANAGEMENT

There is a vast difference between a transactional sale process and strategic account management. In the first process, your approach is weighted towards closing the deal to get the customer to commit to your brand. The purpose of a sales process is to create the most effective route possible for increasing your close rate.

The purpose of strategic account management is to become a trusted advisor to your identified key customer accounts. Strategic account management is about forming a relationship with a customer so that the organization can learn how to drive value for their customer over the long term, not just once with a single sale. In order for an organization to become a trusted advisor, they must have a strategic account management process in place that takes into consideration the following five areas:

1. **Define:** The process begins with a clear definition of what factors identify a key account for the organization. The driving factor cannot just be the current size of the account. A definition for key accounts could be: a select group of customers chosen due to the ongoing mutual value that

can be provided to both parties. In other words, a long-term relationship with a high customer lifetime value.

2. **Drive Value:** The second part of the strategic account management process is about identifying value for the customer. If an organization cannot drive value either now or in the future, there is no need for a relationship. The relationship must be mutually beneficial by providing value for both sides.

3. **Teams:** Transactional sales and buying can be a one-person show on both sides. Key accounts in a strategic account management process will have multiple individuals from both organizations involved. The sales organization must establish a process to assign staff to support the key accounts and identify roles within the key account.

4. **Plan:** Strategic account management is about creating a plan with the customer and keeping that plan current. You and the client are working towards success together; you need a plan to get there.

5. **Perform:** At the end of the day, your organization needs to deliver. The customer journey for key accounts should be flawless. By default, key accounts should have more resources assigned to them, thus having a higher chance of a better experience if the organization's processes work well together.

Strategic account management is dependent on your industry, and takes discipline and dedication to execute well. If done correctly, the customer journey is ongoing, as opposed to one-off or random transactional experiences.

Some believe that e-commerce has led to all customers becoming transactional. I disagree. This belief relies on the mistaken notion that online brands are transactional focused; in fact, they are incredibly customer focused. Consider how Amazon obsesses about their customer experience and makes ongoing suggestions to the consumer. With this over-managed focus, it is no surprise recent *Internet Retailer* data (as of October 2018) shows **Amazon completing 42% of all US e-commerce sales**.

Unfortunately, traditional retail brands treat customers like they are transactional instead of relationship customers. They look at the buyer journey as linear from start to finish. The customer journey, however, doesn't have to be a line. It can be a wheel that goes around and around, with the four stages increasing customer satisfaction with each turn and increasing the customer lifetime value for the brand.

If your intent is to do what is best for the customer, you will form a relationship with your customer to ensure your organization continues to serve them with their best interests in mind. To do that, you need to stay in touch with them and learn about their needs. Referring to a previous example, you need to send them helpful tips about how to start slacklining and suggest what they might need next once they have mastered initial skills, so they can continue their personal journey with your support. Do this, and your organization will have a chance at retaining, and possibly even getting a referral from, your existing customers.

As for referrals, the best way to receive referrals is to simply ask. Set up a process to ask your retained customers in a non-competitive setting. You will be surprised at the results. If you are doing a good enough job to keep some key customers, they are highly likely to recommend you; in fact, they may even become your biggest advocates. Identify these promoters, and leverage what they tell you about what works for them in their dealings with you, and get them to think about who else could benefit from your products and services.

Stage 4
SUMMARY AND REFLECTIONS

SUMMARY

THE LAST STAGE of the customer journey is often the stage that receives the least attention. This is due to linear thinking about the customer journey. If the customer journey is thought of as a revolving wheel, the purpose of the fourth stage is to set up the first stage of the next purchase cycle. Once you have gained a customer, you should do everything you can to retain that customer. Too many brands forget this. New customers are obtained at a cost, while retaining existing customers creates value. According to research done by Bain & Company, **increasing customer retention rates by just 5% can increase profits by 25% to 95%**. It is in your best interest to focus obsessively on this stage!

REFLECTIONS

B2C

- Do you have a process in place to actively retain customers?

- What support could you offer your customers in reaching their goals?

- Do you have an ongoing nurturing campaign?

- Do you ask for referrals?

B2B

- What is your key account management process?

- Do you create plans with your key accounts?

- Are there key account teams established so the relationship doesn't just rest with just one individual?

- Do you ask for referrals?

BRINGING IT ALL TOGETHER: UNDERSTANDING YOUR CUSTOMER JOURNEY

NO MATTER THE type of organization (B2B, B2C, B2A (Any), Non-Profit) these four stages hold true.

Stage 1: Awareness/Consideration: The processes in which a brand creates awareness for their products and services and the "triggering" to cause a consumer to connect and become a lead.

Stage 2: The Sale Process: A consumer moves from uninterested to interested, and all the touchpoints lead up to a conversation with a customer-facing representative which leads to the agreement to purchase a good or service. Once the buyer commits, the after sale process starts.

Stage 3: The After Sale Process: Once the buyer has committed, a new set of processes begin. The after sale process is comprised of payment, delivery, product and/or service orientation, and training. Optimizing this set of processes can mitigate the likelihood of creating a poor touchpoint that sours the entire customer experience.

Stage 4: Retention and Referral: The fourth stage is a set of processes designed to retain customers and gain referrals. This stage often receives the least amount of attention. However, brands should do everything they can to retain customers as opposed to engaging in the enormous efforts most companies put into acquiring customers.

Depending on the industry, the touchpoints will be different. However, no matter the industry, each touchpoint can be positive, neutral, or negative. Touchpoints are all moments of truth for a brand, and every part of the customer journey matters and can be measured.

To serve as an example of how to bring together the four stages of the customer journey, I have analyzed a boutique business that has developed sophisticated processes to create an outstanding customer experience. In this analysis, I am the customer of a barber shop called Barber Ha.

To kick start this observation we'll consider my Net Promoter Score for the organization in question. If you are unfamiliar with the significance of the Net Promoter Score (NPS), it will be covered as a key metric in the next section. As a spoiler, giving a business a nine is being a promoter. Some marketers believe the NPS is the most important metric a business can measure, as it clearly indicates continuance of the relationship and intent for next purchase. The key question in determining an NPS is:

On a scale of 1–10; 1 being the least likely and 10 being the most likely, how likely are you to recommend this brand to friends, family and colleagues?

My score for Barber Ha: 9

I scored Barber Ha at a nine instead of ten because this shop's hipster flair means it will not be right for everyone, but it is damn good, and I promote this barber shop often, which is an unusual customer response in this particular industry.

Like most people, I have developed a personal relationship with everyone who has cut my hair over the years, and have typically followed them from location to location. The *where* (brand) did not matter, but the *who* did. For instance, my first barber cut my hair in my hometown from the time I was three years old, and when I moved away for university, he relocated as well, and so he continued to cut my hair until I moved on. This pattern proceeded right up to my last stylist in Saskatoon, whose relationship with me was so effectively established that she introduced me to my wife. She changed salons, and I followed, and even continued to patronise her when I no longer lived in her area full-time. When she left the industry, I needed a new *person* to cut my hair. I never once thought that I needed a new *place* to get my hair cut. Barber Ha is so good that they overcame my built-in bias.

The brand was able to supplant my previous relationship with the barber/stylist. No fewer than six people in three years have cut my hair at this location. Now, the relationship is the *where*, not the *who*.

How did this happen? How did a brand develop a relationship with me in an industry that traditionally develops tight one-on-one relationships and not brand-to-customer relationships? They did this by creating an amazing customer journey and thus experience, and by recognizing the lifetime value of their best customers.

A TYPICAL CUSTOMER JOURNEY AT BARBER HA:

Stage 1: Awareness/Consideration

I was introduced to Barber Ha by word-of-mouth, but their website was easy to use and I booked my first appointment online. They were recommended, I needed a haircut—done. They have a strong web presence, ranking #1 for the search term, "Barber Shop Edmonton," right after two Yelp results, and their strong and consistent social presence on Facebook and Instagram (1778 followers and 4,333 followers, respectively, at the time of writing). Their web presence follows a consistent theme with tips on style and hair and beard care, plus they genuinely promote other small businesses at their location and via their social presence. Considering I was recommended to them by a small business owner, I suspect one of the biggest drivers of new business for them is referrals.

Stage 2: The Sale Process

Barber Ha has invested in a simple integrated marketing

and customer management online system. Their sale process begins online with an easy-to-use booking system that
begins on the website and is linked to their social presence.
Once you arrive, the customer journey is pleasant and stim-
ulating. The shop has created a mix of a modern look with
an old-time barber shop feel. I find myself entertained just
by looking around at the décor. But when you begin to
walk up to the counter, the magic really starts to happen.
Everyone in the location is genuinely friendly, and they all
seem to know your name. To create this "magic" it is clear to
me they have invested in three things:

1. A simple CRM (customer relationship management)/booking system.

2. Customer Service Training or taking the time to
   build a customer-focused culture.

3. An Integrated Tech Stack: Web, CRM, Accounting
   tied together.

INSIGHT

INTEGRATED TECH STACK DEFINITION

An Integrated Tech Stack is a general catch-all term
used for management information systems that work
together to share data and updates simultaneously.
Most enterprise-level organizations strive to have

their Marketing and Marketing Automation software, Customer Relationship Management software, and Enterprise Resource Planning software (accounting, purchasing, inventory, scheduling, production) all work as one. While at first glance this may appear to be exclusively be the domain of medium to large enterprises, for smaller enterprises, the theory equally holds as the technology does not have to be complex. Since everything is moving to cloud computing, it is easy to integrate marketing and customer relationship management software, even on the small enterprise scale of a barber shop. The accounting software may not be linked in all cases, including at Barber Ha. Nonetheless, they have created a seamless experience for the customer.

These investments create the following outcomes.

No fewer than two staff will say hello to you using your name before you sit down and wait. This makes me feel welcome, and I feel they care about who I am. I cannot recall another salon or barber shop where my first name was used consistently by anyone other than the person cutting my hair; at this barber shop, a minimum of six different staff members have said hello to me using my first name during my visits.

They run a tight ship. The haircut process is efficient and always on time, and as such, they enforce a strict no show policy that is executed without compromise but comes across with consideration. This is how they do it: a reminder email and phone call occurs prior to each appointment. If you are not there five minutes prior to your appointment, they call to ensure you can still make it on time. So they remind you enough times that you understand if you are late it is clearly your fault, and they have done everything they could to help you to be on time. If you are too late you get bumped, because they will not punish the next customer because you cannot show up on time. I appreciate this because I never get told they are running behind. I walk in, sit down, often right in the barber chair, and get my hair cut efficiently, expertly, and in a friendly manner.

Stage 3: The After Sale Process

When your haircut is complete, you are escorted to the counter to pay. You are asked genuinely if the hair cut turned out the way you wanted. There is a product upsell and the next appointment is booked. They thank you for your business, and often several people wave goodbye or say, "See you, Steve!" or "Have a good day!" I walk out feeling great after every cut because of how I have been treated. My positive experiences seem representative, as they have received hundreds of online reviews and are currently rated at 4.8 out of 5 on Google.

Stage 4: Retention and Referral

Their outstanding service creates referrals and positive review ratings, but they have never asked if I knew anyone that could use their services, so I suspect they limit their referral process through the co-promotion of other small businesses.

It appears that this is working, but an actual B2C referral program might bring in additional business, as would an automated continual customer contact. Their customer contact is limited to automated reminder emails from their booking system. They do have a prepaid program that is nice, as it incorporates a discount. This is clearly smart retention, as the brand gets a commitment from the customer for up to a year, which guarantees return business—or an amazing ROI on unused services!

Conclusion

Overall, Barber Ha provides a great customer experience that takes no more than a little bit of creative décor, a decent CRM/booking software, disciplined processes, and a staff that genuinely tries to know and be friendly and courteous to all clients, not just the client whose hair they cut.

If a barber shop can manage the four stages with excellence, what is stopping you? Anyone can do this. It's simply a matter of mapping your customer journey and designing a process that creates an amazing customer experience.

Once mapped and understood, the measurement of critical customer journey touchpoints fosters real transformation and growth. The next section dives into KPIs critical for improving the customer journey.

Section Two
MEASURING THE CUSTOMER JOURNEY

MANY EXPERTS CLAIM that creating a great customer experience is simple, you just need to genuinely care about your customer. If it's so simple, why are so many brands now failing? Perhaps it is because they did not gather objective facts to measure their customer journey. **Case in point: 80% of companies believe they deliver superior customer service, but only 8% of people believe these same companies deliver superior customer service** (source: Lee Resources). This massive disconnect occurs because the customer journey is not being measured and assessed as a whole.

Understanding most processes requires the ability to accurately measure them. This goes backs to the old adage: what gets measured, gets managed. In this "customer age," developing the capacity to measure and then manage your customer's journey for optimization is the key to success. Capturing data, understanding data, creating insights from data, and applying these insights to your organization, if done well and consistently, provides a competitive advantage.

Perhaps when considering measurement, the ultimate question is which ratios and KPIs should be measured? Which metrics will make a difference? I personally can cite over 50 business metrics off the top of my head. There are hundreds more to consider. In the organizations I have served, either as an executive, board member, or vendor, only a handful need to be measured to make a difference.

If creating the ultimate customer journey is the key to success, and in order to improve towards that success you need to measure it, what then, are the simple metrics that matter for measuring the customer journey? The four stages of the customer journey can be measured and improved upon through eight critical KPIs of your organization.

Over the course of this section will we dive into the eight key metrics, that when put together create a framework that can transform an organization's results when they are measured and combined with continuous improvement. Let us first define and explain what each metric showcases in your business and why that metric is important. The eight metrics are as follows:

1. Total Advertising Reach
2. Conversion Rate
3. Lead Count
4. Close Rate
5. Revenue Metrics
6. Reputation Management
7. Net Promoter Score
8. Churn Rate

As you can see in "The Metric Wheel", when the customer journey is represented as wheel, not as a progressive linear journey with an end, a framework for continuous engagement is created. Your customer can either continue on with your organization and do another lap on the wheel, or, if the stages are handled poorly they can veer off toward another organization.

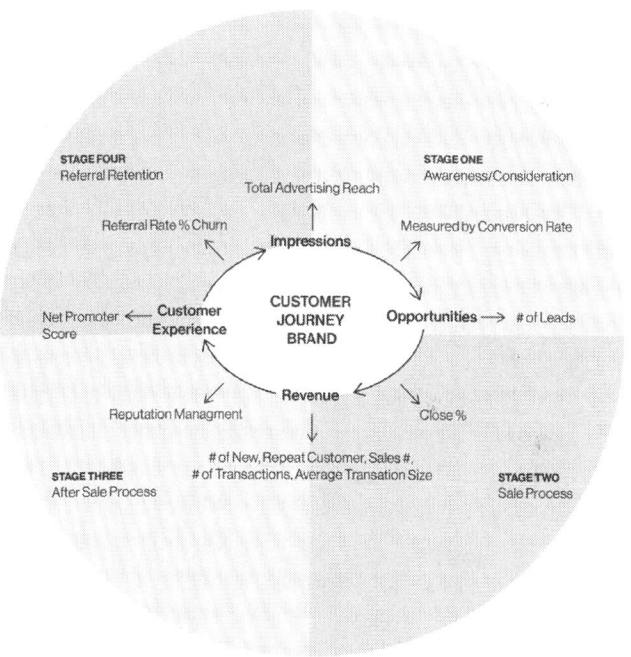

Download this graphic and more at stevewhittington.com

B2B organizations that practice strategic account management coupled with account-based marketing have long understood this. The opportunity for most brands today (whether B2B, B2C, or B2A) is to think along similar lines.

BEST PRACTICE

ACCOUNT-BASED MARKETING

Account-based marketing refers to marketing to one instead of marketing to many. Current digital technology has promised the mass personalization of marketing efforts for marketing teams, but personalization is still only the first step. Account-based marketing is the complete integration of sales and marketing in organizations that use strategic account management. It is an ongoing and evolving marketing effort on a per-account basis.

The core elements of account-based marketing are quite similar to strategic account management, except with a marketing flair. The intent is to engage the prospect (or continue to engage a current client) with specific content for that account, in an effort to provide value to that account. Delivery of content is also specific to that account. The steps for account-based marketing are as follows:

1. Select key accounts.

2. Create an individual marketing plan for each key account.

3. Create specific content that provides value for each key account.

4. Determine the most effective channels on a per-account basis.

5. Execute targeted and coordinated (with sales and all channels) campaigns.

6. Measure, learn, and optimize.

Organizations that use account-based marketing have seen a higher ROI on their marketing efforts, which makes sense due to the concentration of effort onto an individual account.

This is marketing that is personalized by channel and effort for each account. Providing information that is relevant to and valued by the account for each step of their customer journey is a complete departure from the traditional one-to-many marketing approach.

Every new customer provides an opportunity to create a lifetime customer and a key account. An organization must shift from linear customer journey thinking to circular or continuous customer journey thinking. The Disney Institute, in their teachings of customer experience, allude to this, indicating that all journeys add up to an aggregate experience, and that each journey is linked.

The customers first experience becomes their context or baseline

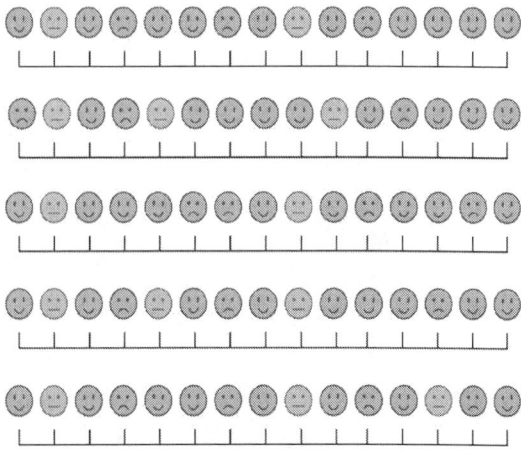

You can build up a reservoir of good or bad will over time

Download this graphic and more at stevewhittington.com

In this diagram, each line represents a customer experience (or journey) within an organization. Each dot represents a touchpoint. **A touchpoint refers to your brand's interactions with a customer during any time in the customer journey, from end to end.** For example, a touchpoint could be a social media post, radio ad, online review, website, store signage, in store greeting, interaction with staff, purchasing, use of product or receiving of service, thank you cards, warranty, ongoing marketing emails … to name just a few. Over time, the bad touchpoints (red) and neutral touchpoints (yellow) compile, and will push a customer beyond the point of return, which is why every touchpoint matters.

That said, plenty of research points to the fact that organizations do not get much more than one chance; in fact 26% of customers only give one chance.

> "Of almost 1,000 consumers polled, 92% say they would stop purchasing from a company after three or fewer poor customer service experiences. Twenty-six percent of those would stop after just one bad experience."

-Gladly's *2018*

Customer Service Expectations Survey

With only one chance to get it right, every critical stage of the customer journey must be monitored to be able to optimize or immediately apply corrective action.

So let's dive into the metrics that matter.

Stage 1
AWARENESS/CONSIDERATION

IN THIS STAGE, the customer or client is becoming aware of your organization and your organization's ability to meet their needs. As described in Section One, awareness can be triggered in different ways depending on the industry, products, or services. Some organizations rely just on repeat business and word of mouth; whereas others conduct extensive acquisition marketing such as online and print ads, direct response mail, tradeshows, and radio offers to obtain leads. The Awareness/Consideration stage metrics measure how much and where the awareness is coming from, which awareness activities are converting, and thus how leads are obtained. By measuring and optimizing these metrics, you can increase the total organizational opportunity.

KPI #1: Reach

Reach is a measurement of the total number of potential and current customers or clients (impressions) who are exposed to your offering during a given time period. A typical time period can be a month or a week, but depending on the business and marketing campaign conducted, some campaigns' time periods are just days or even hours. Measuring traditional media buys and obtaining digital impressions is an easy place to start. However, there are other factors to consider, such as organizational awareness-generating activities such as emails sent, organizational physical presence (location signage, company vehicles, branded customer equipment), prospecting customer touches, and customer word-of-mouth. Some of these can be empirically measured; others require an informed estimate. However, defining a time period and measuring the total reach during the time period X is the first metric to gather and measure within your customer journey.

What does this KPI tell us? It tells us how much total promotional activity a brand is doing. Importantly, this data needs to be segmented by channel, so the brand knows the impressions per channel. To complete this exercise, all the channels need to be tied back to a budget or spend during time period X. Anchoring the reach of a channel to a budget (either labour invested, or media buy) lets you know the cost of your promotional activity for each channel.

BEST PRACTICE

HOW TO MEASURE REACH

The easiest way to measure your organization's reach is to start by listing all the channels that are in use in efforts to increase attention to your brand. This includes all traditional media buys for advertising. Also consider reviewing website traffic, social impressions, and other forms of contact such as trade show traffic, sales team account calling, and more—as granular as you wish to make it. The important thing is for you to start to measure the channels you use that matter to your customers.

A simple way to start, without having to pay for business intelligence dashboards, is to use Excel spreadsheets. Record your channels, pick a time period (most organizations use monthly), and document the cost per channel. Your costs will be easy to acquire as they fall into three categories: ad buy/production costs, creative costs and distribution costs.

The ad buy is just that, the cost of the ad buy for a channel, though there may be production costs associated with the channel such as a billboard signage or the printing costs for a flyer if conducting a direct mail campaign.

Creative costs can be a flat fee or an hourly cost per ad from either an outside agency or your internal team.

Distribution costs are usually the cost of mailing, but could also include other delivery methods of awareness such as the cost of "brand ambassadors" for an experiential campaign.

As an example of how to calculate costs, for a print

ad there will be the ad placement cost plus creative design costs, which together will give you a true total cost. For a direct mail offer, you need to include creative design costs, production costs, and distribution costs (targeted mailing). For a social media post there will be creative costs and channel distribution costs (if paying/boosting for more than organic reach). Be sure to document all costs so that a true total cost by channel can be achieved.

Once the costs per channel are recorded, you need to know what the reach is. Digital is easy, as analytics provide impressions for the time period you query. Traditional is relatively straightforward as well, as pressure from digital has forced traditional media to provide numbers. Print ads have a distribution provided on a per-issue basis; that is your reach for that channel. Billboards can provide reasonable estimates of car traffic per day; that is the base measurement from which to estimate your reach; direct mail provides detailed delivery receipts; those are your reach. With a little planning, it thus becomes possible to either actually measure reach or create a very reasonable estimate. With your cost and reach recorded on a per-channel basis, you have enabled yourself to calculate critical KPIs for the first part of the customer journey.

While I have written this as a simple process, having gone through it internally at organizations and with many clients, it does require a shift in thinking. Instead of just buying ads, you are now conducting "Marketing Math" on every channel. This means you are really beginning to assess with objectivity instead of subjectivity. The old adage, "half of my advertising works, I just don't know which half" is 100% unacceptable with the tools available to organizations today. It takes discipline and time to gather all the data, but once it's done, you have your first tool.

Why is this important? By going through the exercise of measuring all your channels for reach and cost, you have **your first basic comparison data point: cost per impression (CPI)**. Cost per impression is calculated by dividing the total cost by the number of impressions during time period t.

CPI = Total Cost/Total Impressions (during time period t)

CPI = $5600/10,000 = $0.56 per impression

This data is helpful, as it can inform budget allocations. If the cost per impression is significantly lower on one channel versus another channel, the budget can be applied or restricted to increase or reduce attention for the brand. As a marketer buying media, this is the first basic metric I look at when evaluating channels: "what is the cost per impression," or "what is my bang for my buck?" No matter the industry, using this metric to rank your channels is an objective measurement that sets up KPI #2: Conversion Rate.

Marketing Channel ROI - Template

CHANNEL	COST				ATTRIBUTION		
	Ad Buy/ Production	Creative	Distribution	Total Cost	Impressions	CPI	Conversion Rate
Billboard	$5,000.00	$350.00		$5,350.00	75,000	$0.07	
Print Ad	$4,200.00	$350.00		$4,550.00	36,000	$0.13	
Ad Words	$5,000.00	$150.00		$5,150.00	61,000	$0.00	
Direct Mail	$12,500.00	$2,500.00	$3,200.00	$18,200.00	45,000	$0.40	

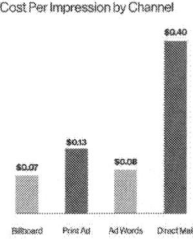

Cost Per Impression by Channel

Download this graphic and more at stevewhittington.com

The generic example above showcases how to evaluate CPI per channel. As you become more detailed, these channels can be further segmented to increase insights. For instance, there will be a different CPI per publication in print that an organization uses. In the example above, Billboards and AdWords incur the lowest cost per impression. So, if you are seeking to increase the awareness of a product or a new initiative for your organization, these channels may deserve more spend. However, if your goals are to convert your offer into dollars, you will need the insight of KPI #2: Conversion Rate to help guide you. All the eyeballs in the world mean nothing if nobody buys.

KPI #2: Conversation Rate

The conversion rate is a simple ratio determined by the number of leads obtained divided by the reach of a channel. For instance, a typical online conversion rate is 2.5%. This is calculated by the number of leads or sales obtained from your website divided by visitors to your website in a set time period (typically a month).

FORMULA

250 leads from site/10,000 monthly website visitors
= Conversion rate of 2.5%

To ensure this conversion rate is accurate, you must track your leads obtained per each channel. KPI #3 will provide more details on this process, as tracking leads is a practice in of itself that can be accomplished through call accounting; UTM codes for digital ads or leads by source from a CRM. Your organization's CRM can provide you with a very important data set. In order for it to be accurate, however, the customer-facing staff will need education on the organization's marketing data needs.

INSIGHT

UTM, URL, CRM, A/B TESTING

UTM Codes: A UTM (Urchin Tracking Module) code is a simple code that you can attach to a custom URL (Uniform Resource Locator) in your web address in order to track the source, medium, and campaign name. This enables Google Analytics to tell you where searchers came from as well as what campaign directed them to you. To understand this process in more depth the best resource is Google Analytics Academy https://analytics.google.com/analytics/academy/. The courses are quick, and provide interactive demos and assessments to verify the learning.

CRM: Customer Relationship Management software systems are focused on capturing all interactions an organization has with customers. Many CRMs are highly adaptable, allowing them to meet the unique needs and unique measurement requirements of individual organizations. They have also been moving away from being an independent software system, rather they are now being fully integrated with marketing automation and financial systems. This integration allows for virtually real-time ROI and lead attribution on sales and marketing activities, as long as the data recorded is accurate.

A/B Testing is a method of comparing two versions of a webpage, ad, landing page, or app against the other to determine which one performs (converts) better. Best practice methodology confines the changes to one or two changes per ad version in order to ensure a clear understanding of which change created the impact.

What does this KPI tell us? With the conversion rate measured, you have comparison data for each of your channels, while with the previous metric you could track cost per impression. With the conversation rate, you will know cost per lead and conversion rate per channel. Arguably, the purpose of marketing is to create leads, so knowing this metric is vital.

Why is this important? Knowing clearly what works and what does not work allows a marketer to funnel funding effectively and to objectively review a campaign's effectiveness. This data allows for A/B testing, offer optimization, and channel cost effectiveness comparison based on results, not just mass reach. As a marketer, **if you can move your conversation rate up, you can increase your organization's total opportunity, but you need to know it before you can improve it.**

INSIGHT

LEARNING WHAT WORKS

Often, the start of a customer journey is contact with, or exposure to a promotional activity, or landing page on the organization's website. By measuring each offer, ad, landing page, channel, and social platform and learning the conversion rate for each, you will know what works and doesn't work for your organization.

Or will you? You can quickly learn what didn't convert based on the set of circumstances in which you used the channel. Note that the conversion rate is a lagging indicator. You are looking through the rearview mirror into the past to determine what to do in the future.

This learning process is not as black and white as the metric makes it seem. You need to glean insights from the metric. Consider the following scenarios.

Low conversion rate:	0.001 or 0.1%
Average conversion rate:	0.025 or 2.5%
High conversion rate:	0.095 or 9.5%

With these three numbers, it would seem obvious what you should do. However, the numbers do not tell the whole story without further context.

Let's look at a couple of real-world examples:

Scenario One

My team was reviewing the weekly KPIs on a currently running ad campaign; we call this our health check. The marketing team runs the KPIs weekly and reviews the results with the sales team to determine next steps based on what is occurring in a campaign. One campaign was for an agricultural product. The team member showcased the results and how the conversion rate had dramatically fallen in the previous week across all channels. The first conclusion was to consider that the campaign for this product was nearing its end—perhaps the seasonality of the product ended sooner than expected. This was a fair assumption to make, without looking deeper into the context.

Here is the context: The current harvest in western Canada had been challenging due to weather. In some places, the harvest had started and stopped three or more times. The week in which the drop in conversion rate occurred represented the first stretch of good weather (it was 8 days long) in over 40 days. The farmers ran to the fields and stayed in them for 16 hours a day in an attempt to get their crop off the fields. They were not concerned with buying a piece of used equipment or tillage equipment that week. Their attention was elsewhere.

With that context provided, there was a collective "ahh!" in the room. The next week the conversion rate returned to regular campaign levels.

On the flip side, you need to be equally suspicious of high conversion rates. What is going on that initiates the spike? Generally, there is some outside context driving the behavior, either that or your offer is so underpriced that you have left money on the table.

Scenario Two

Evaluating channels: Be prepared to question your own influence along with the channel's effectiveness. A common trap that occurs when evaluating channels is to whitewash the effectiveness of the channel based on the results provided. For instance, when evaluating a print publication with a low conversion rate, one can conclude that the channel doesn't convert. But what about the offer being presented? How good (or bad) was your creative? What about the ad placement within the publication? I have had conversion rates increase by moving an ad either nearer to the front of the publication or to the back page; I have also had ad conversion rates increase by changing the layout of the ad, and counter intuitively "doubling down" in one scenario, when a single page spread was converting at best average, but when a two page spread was purchased, the conversion rate spiked due to the impact the ad had on the body of the publication.

The point to all these scenarios is that a single metric can only be a guide or a flag for further investigation and thinking, not a gatekeeper, and certainly these metrics need to be combined with additional results in order to understand the whole story. When picking new channels, you will need to include a broader context, beyond the expected conversion rate, in order to evaluate your desired outcomes.

KPI #3: Leads

The purpose of marketing is to create opportunity; for most organizations, opportunity equals leads. In order to calculate KPI #2: Conversion, you need to be tracking all leads, which is a basis for KPI #4: Close Rate.

To measure this KPI, the definition of a lead needs to be clear for your organization. I generically define a lead as follows: **a lead is a prospect that has taken an action that shows purchase intent**. A prospect that does this will most likely have a need, a reason, and/or interest in pursuing your product or service. To be fair, this is a broad, catch-all definition.

The segmentation of leads and sub definitions can get quite detailed. For instance, is a customer inquiring for more information about a product on your website considered a lead? Does a request for product information show buying intent? I believe so, but the prospect may just be starting to research and evaluate a product. It is the organization's job to provide the proper support to the prospect to nurture them along their buying journey. Similarly, when an individual makes a phone call or physically enters a place of business, do you consider them a lead? Again, I believe so. By and large, customers do not go out of their way to call or enter most business without some sort of intent. As for their readiness to buy and timing, however, that is a different set of questions.

Contrary to the broad definition above, some organizations do not consider an inquiry a lead unless it includes a request for a quote. Depending on the industry, what gets handed to sales as a *qualified* lead depends on the buyer behavior in that industry and the nuances of the organization's sale process.

INSIGHT

UNDERSTANDING LEAD CLASSIFICATIONS

The typical classification of leads in B2B follows a waterfall model, starting with a Marketing Collected Lead (MCL) that becomes Qualified (MQL), which is then handed off to Sales (SQL), who determines whether the lead is ready to be sold to, and if so, then the organization has a real ready-to-buy opportunity. The four typical stages of a lead are as follows:

1. (MCL) Marketing Collected Lead: A lead collected by marketing activities that has not yet been qualified.

2. (MQL) Marketing Qualified Lead: A lead that marketing collected and then qualified. The typical requirements for qualification follow the acronym BANT:

Budget: Is there a budget in place to purchase the good or service?

Authority: Does the contact have purchasing authority?

Need: Is there a business challenge that the good or service solves?

Timeframe: When is the product or service needed? Is this known?

3. (SQL) Sales Qualified Lead: Sales now begins to work with the prospect to determine the readiness to buy. If the lead is determined to be ready to buy within the organization's typical sales cycle time frame, the SQL becomes an opportunity.

4. Opportunity: A sales qualified lead that has a defined timeline for purchase.

Depending on the organization, this can be a long, detailed process that is handled by multiple individuals, or, as is often the case with B2C industries, the process can be compressed into a single phone call or web inquiry. As an organization, you need to create your definition of a qualified lead and continue to refine it based on your sale process needs.

With the definition of a lead clarified, leads then need to be gathered and measured. Online form submissions are the first place to start—this is an easy tally. Online chat and social media can also capture leads through conversations that draw out prospects and pass them to sales. All digital forms are easy to measure, using UTM codes that allow for unique tracking measurement. Call tracking numbers can also be used with print or digital ads, by creating unique call tracking numbers for each ad or publication, as well as call counting at physical locations and head count monitoring systems for physical traffic. Finally, an effectively utilized CRM closes the loop with source attribution. The key is to become obsessive about capturing all leads. Too often, legitimate business opportunities are dismissed. If all leads were captured, measured, and worked, where do you think your business would go?

It is estimated that only 4% of marketing-generated leads actually close. So, where does the other 96% go? Even if half of the leads that fall off never had any intention of buying from any organization, there is still a tremendous amount of opportunity to be captured. That can only happen if all leads are tracked and measured.

BEST PRACTICE

TRACKING LEADS

Tracking leads requires planning, coding, systems, and software. As a marketer, when you are planning a promotion and writing a creative brief, beyond the offer, creative elements, production, and channel selection, you need to determine how you are going to track attribution. As daunting as this may seem, there are really just six main ways to track leads and thereby provide attribution for your marketing. When broken down, they become easy to do. The six ways are:

1. Digital Tracking
2. Call Tracking
3. Redeemable Offer/Promotion
4. CRM
5. Event Capture
6. Traffic Counts

Digital Tracking

Through the use of UTM codes, attribution for actions that happen online can be tracked using your website analytics, from the source all the way to the last action taken online, which hopefully is lead conversion. I will not dive into the specifics and best practices around UTM code use, as they are simple to use and create and should employ a standard naming convention. What is important is to define what represents a conversion for goal tracking online (is it a form-submission-like request quote, click to call? or just downloading a current offer sheet?) and establishing a reporting procedure to quickly determine the number of leads. Limitations with UTM codes lead us to call tracking.

Call Tracking

When combined with UTM codes, call tracking provides a marketer and analyst with a powerful tool set combination. Each specific ad can have a separate call tracking number. Your website can be coded to refresh with new tracking numbers depending on the source from which the visitor arrived. Having call tracking numbers on all channels creates crystal clarity on what generates results. Your business may not generate leads through phone calls; if that is the case, this tactic will not be as important to you. But even understanding the volume of calls with ongoing business can be an insight in itself. I know of many businesses that instituted call tracking and, within a few weeks, were able to understand how to improve their customer experience. They reviewed call volume and assigned additional resources during peak times.

They also listened to recorded calls to glean insights on process improvements. A simple function such as incoming calls required assessment with "new eyes," and when supported by facts, the conclusion of these assessments was clear, and could be measured when changes were employed.

Redeemable Offer/Promotion

The classic coupon is still a great way to track leads. Of course, with current tools a coupon now comes in many forms, from discount codes online to a sales code presented at physical point of sale. A specific offer is easy to track, however, as a customer needs only to mention the promotion and it can be entered at the point of sale for it to be tracked. The challenge with creating an offer within an integrated media buy is to determine which channel brought the customer in for the offer. If the same message is on Facebook, radio, and print, and the customer enters a location because of the item on sale, which media channel brought them in? That is where the CRM comes in.

CRM

When the sales team is capturing a lead, an easy question to ask is, "What brought you in today or prompted you to call?" The customer will generally let you know, "I heard your ad on the radio," or "I saw the promotion on Facebook." If your sales team asks the question and records the data diligently, and if your organization has a CRM that can record lead attribution, this tool can be one of your best sources, and will subsequently act as a cross reference to your other data sets.

Event Capture

At events for customers, captured leads can be recorded at the event or immediately afterwards and be easily attribution qualified. The key, of course, is for your sales team to capture leads at the events.

Traffic Counts

There are two types of traffic counts that can be recorded: online and physical store interactions (either call volume or foot traffic). For your website, Google Analytics is free, and the software allows you to make annotations to timestamp events (such as when a radio campaign started). With either online or physical store interactions when media channels are used that do not provide easy to track attribution (such as billboards, TV or radio), look for a spike in your traffic. For instance if your website traffic spikes when you begin a TV campaign, and thus your calls from the website increases, this is an important factor to be aware of.

Lead Attribution

In today's multiple screen, multimedia world, which

channel gets credit for the lead? A customer can hear a radio ad, see a post on a social platform on their phone, drive past the store, and then go directly to the website and buy a product online or call the location. In this scenario, to which channel do you attribute the lead? Some marketers ascribe to last touch attribution; others apportion a percentage of credit to each channel. I personally default to last touch attribution, but seek to understand all factors. In the TV example, I would look at multiple sources: web traffic changes, store traffic changes, CRM lead attribution, and leads generated from the website (calls or inquiry forms). Generally, more than one channel made an impact in order to cause the stimulus for the customer to act.

Figuring this out can be a riddle, but one worth solving in order to learn what works and what doesn't.

What does this KPI tell us? Knowing the quantity of leads that come in by channel allows cost per lead to be calculated for each channel. Also, with the help of metrics from the next stage (close percentage; average transaction size), the ROI by channel can be calculated. At the end of the day, knowing the total number of leads coming into your organization allows you to understand your total new business potential.

Why is this important? Knowing the performance of each channel allows a marketer to determine where to funnel ad dollars for optimization; furthermore, knowing the total quantity of leads generated showcases an organization's opportunity and sets the stage for measuring the next KPI, Close Rate, which indicates how much of that opportunity is being captured.

As another layer of understanding is added, the picture changes. Consider when only the cost per impression was known about a channel. Based off that metric, a billboard buy appeared to be the best value. However, when KPI #3: Leads was added, a new conclusion could be reached. Based on the cost per lead calculated below, the billboard channel now would appear to provide the least value, at $214.00, of the channels tracked, versus $52.55 per lead for AdWords. However, this is the not whole story, as you will see when we dive into tracking Stage 2: The Sale Process.

STEVE WHITTINGTON

Marketing Channel ROI - Template

| CHANNEL | COST | | | | ATTRIBUTION | | | | |
	Ad Buy/ Production	Creative	Distribution	Total Cost	Impressions	CPI	Conversion Rate	Leads	Cost Per Lead
Billboard	$5,000.00	$350.00		$5,350.00	75,000	$0.07	0.03%	25	$214.00
Print Ad	$4,200.00	$350.00		$4,550.00	36,000	$0.13	0.13%	47	$96.81
Ad Words	$5,000.00	$150.00		$5,150.00	61,000	$0.08	0.16%	98	$52.55
Direct Mail	$12,500.00	$2,500.00	$3,200.00	$18,200.00	45,000	$0.40	0.32%	145	$125.52

Cost Per Impression by Channel

Cost Per Lead

Download this graphic and more at stevewhittington.com

Stage 1
SUMMARY AND REFLECTIONS

SUMMARY

IF YOU ARE a marketing and sales professional, by now you will note that Stage 1: Awareness/Consideration is just another name for the top of the traditional funnel, in which a brand creates attention for the product or service to the customer, who then goes on to the research and consideration phase of their buying journey. There are books and SAAS (Software-as-a-Service) platforms dedicated to just this part of the customer journey. The details, mapping, and metrics can be intense and deep. The scope of this section is to launch you on your journey to gather metrics and then apply them to objective business decisions.

With less than 30% of businesses currently tracking ROI on their marketing activities, the first key point is to just start, keep it simple, and learn some easy insights that can have profound impacts on your business. For instance, what if you learned by call tracking that a monthly recurring ad you have been running for your business creates basically no calls, and then further, you could not qualify walk in traffic nor web traffic as a result of the ad. Would it be worthwhile to stop the ad for a few months and save your business several thousand dollars to see if there is any impact? Or what if another promotion you are running is getting plenty of attention (impressions) but no conversions? What is wrong? Wrong audience, wrong offer?

Keeping the tracking simple can open up substantial opportunity for understanding and improvement. Begin tracking your activities that create stimulus for consumer action and learn what works and doesn't work.

REFLECTIONS/ACTION ITEMS

- List the channels on which you conduct promotional activities. Do any of them need to be segmented? Use the worksheet provided at stevewhittington.com to record these channels.

- Record the total cost per channel. If you have an internal staff member working on the creative, make sure you add in an hourly rate for their time.

- Record the impressions per channel. Now you have KPI #1: Reach.

- Calculate Cost Per Impression (CPI). Record your observations. Are there any insights gained from this step?

- Do you have an agreed-upon definition of a lead? If

not, create one and use it as a standard for measuring what is a lead and what is not a lead.

- What are you currently doing to track leads? Write down what you have in place now. Reflect on your channels. Are there gaps? If so, what can you do to measure processes currently in place to fill in your data gaps? Create a plan to fill in the gaps, but start with what you have. Any insights are better than no insights. Record the leads by channel. Then calculate the cost per lead.

- Now what have you learned? Record your reflections.

Stage 2
THE SALE PROCESS

THE SALE PROCESS begins when there's contact between a prospect and a brand representative who can sell or provide a product or service. Essentially, this is when a request received by an organization is acted upon. The effectiveness of this stage is measured by the close rate and revenue KPIs. Total revenue by itself is not an effective KPI. Many organizations focus obsessively on top line revenue, but the juice is in the details. KPIs within revenue such as new customers versus existing customers, average transaction size, and customer lifetime value tell a more complete story of the total revenue. These KPIs within revenue are needed in order to provide a true understanding of other KPIs in the customer journey. In this section, I will dive deeper into each KPI. However, focusing on revenue metrics before understanding an organization's close rate is like counting your chickens before they hatch.

KPI #4: Close Rate

The close rate is the percentage of incoming leads that convert into commercial transactions. The biggest challenge

to calculating this metric for most companies is in tracking all incoming leads and defining what constitutes a lead. As detailed in the previous section, leads need to be clearly defined and obsessively tracked. Without objective measurement, you have only biased opinions to work from. Sales team members will often claim 40–50% close rates, while industry statistic after industry statistic claims that 80% of leads are not closed. Why this disconnect? The disconnect comes in an organization's customer-facing staff customer qualifying process.

A common sales team objection to the "80% of leads never convert" statistic is that the leads are no good. The leads are "tire kickers." Thus, they claim a 40–50% close rate on *qualified* opportunities, which are buyers near the end of the buying funnel. If all leads are quantified and classified as *qualified* (a prospect that has taken an action showing purchase intent) as opposed to prospects that show clear buying signals and are 100% *qualified*, a true close percentage will occur, and opportunity to improve will be illuminated.

INSIGHT

CLOSING THE 80% GAP

The first challenge to increasing an organization's close percentage often starts at the very beginning of the process, when the organization initially engages a prospect. As detailed in the four steps to follow in a phone lead, the challenge is in getting the sales team to capture the lead. The first part of that example showcases a typical customer interaction, an interaction in which the customer (a lead) contacted the organization, but the organization's sales team did not capture any information. Because the lead was not captured, a debate will occur as to whether the customer was able to be advanced as a qualified lead or not. Marketing via tracking may record that a lead occurred, but in this case, sales will not have entered the lead into the sales funnel because it wasn't captured. Thus, there is a gap between marketing leads and sales qualified leads.

The first way to start to bridge this gap is to implement a sale process. With a sale process in place, you can start to track the percentage of progress from your marketing generated leads to sales qualified leads. If the gap decreases, the process is making a difference.

Process and training together can make a difference. But process, training, or coaching alone has been proven to only create productivity increases of 4%. However, with process, training, and coaching combined, there have been up to 88% increases recorded, and on average 17% increases occur with three hours per month of coaching, according to the Sales Executive Council.

Why this massive difference? Processes do not drive

behaviour and intent. You can execute processes with an ineffective intent.

If your intent is to get the customer their answers and move on, you will have a far different outcome than if your intent is to solve their problem and listen to their needs.

So you need to coach your team on processes. How do you do that? The same way all professional athletes are coached: by reviewing game tape. Except your game tape for transactional interactions will be reviewing emails sent, chat engine transcripts, and recorded calls; for customers you have converted to accounts, the number of account touches can be reviewed, as well as the status of key account plans, and documented correspondence.

In today's world there are many ways to provide "on the court" data to use to coach your team to improve. When reality is regularly showcased and deviations from a proven sale process are evident, there is no debate about whether the lead is good or not. The debate is gone. It is replaced with a desire to learn how to improve.

INSIGHT

CHALLENGES OF IMPLEMENTING CALL RECORDING

If an organization has not provided transparent feedback before, there can be some hesitation on the part of the staff as to how to receive feedback. However, it has been my experience that as long as the intent of the data being gathered is for improvement, as opposed to being used to ensure strict conformity and as a tool for reprimands, the information will be well received. Reviewing your customer journey live can actually be quite illuminating. Listening to customer sales calls will quickly showcase sale process missteps and product knowledge gaps.

The "game tape" gathered is not just for your sales team. Listening to general recorded calls other than sales calls can let your support teams know which actions they are taking that are detracting from the customer journey. A simple example is to ensure reception is carefully qualifying the customer for the proper department. It may be surprising to learn how many calls are routed to the wrong department due to assumptions made by a receptionist. For instance, if a customer calls in looking for information about part X, is this a parts department call or a service call? A simple clarifying question can save a misrouting and the poor touchpoint for the customer. When you are listening to recorded calls and the customer is routed to the wrong department, when they think no one is listening, they sure let you know!

If the calls are reviewed regularly with staff, they present an amazing learning tool. If you are going to record calls, be sure to review the legislation for your area to ensure you conform to legal requirements.

What does this tell us? An organization's or individual's close percentage tells us so many things, but first and foremost it identifies how much additional opportunity an organization or individual has. If 80 out of 100 leads are going elsewhere, there is an immediate four-fold growth opportunity—without requiring any additional acquisition marketing!

Consider this scenario: A typical action taken to increase revenue is to increase advertising. However, taking the above example, why not obsessively focus on lead management and your close rate as opposed to buying more attention? As an example, we will use $1,000 as the average transaction size. If the margin on each transaction is 40%, $400 of gross margin contribution can be gained. If this organization is typical, 80 out of 100 of leads are going elsewhere or, in this scenario, $32,000 of gross margin contribution. If this happens in a week, and this is the number of leads per salesperson, and an organization has five sales people, this number adds up fast.

What if instead of buying an ad for $1,000 per week, the organization focused on increasing the close rate and captured just 10% more of that $32,000? The weekly gross margin contribution (GMC) would increase from $8,000 to $11,200 solely by just capturing eight more sales, or a little over one more per day. If the close rate stayed the same, the organization would have to bring in 11 more sales (8 sales + 3 to pay for the ad) just to break even with the tactic of focusing on increasing the close rate. Again, if we consider that the close rate stayed the same, the $1,000 ad would have to provide 55 more leads to produce these 11 sales, or an increase of 55%, to the current lead volume. So which tactic sounds easier and more sustainable? Increase the close rate by 10% or increase the lead volume by 55%?

Why is this important? Measuring your close percentage presents a quick metric that can be improved upon immediately, and is one that will directly and immediately affect your bottom line. With sales training and ongoing sales coaching, quick gains can be made. While this KPI is part of the customer journey metric, it is also a people metric. By knowing each salesperson's close rate, you can quickly identify individuals that need support. The close rate can uncover opportunity areas that a high sales volume could be masking. As a result, each individual on the sales team can immediately improve both their business and the organization's customer journey.

In addition, when the close rate is known, projecting the ROI for marketing activities becomes possible. For instance, when the conversion rate (KPI #2) for reach (KPI #1) is known, and thus the number of leads (KPI #3) that will be generated can be calculated, with a known close rate (KPI #4) the total projected sales calculations are now possible—and therefore your ROI.

KPI #5: Revenue

The question that is always asked in business circles is: How's business? The answer is usually a derivative of sales: "Business is good—we are experiencing double-digit sales growth." That is a simple ten-word answer that does not give any understanding as to why or how sales have gone up or down. Revenue is an outcome of activities completed before the sale, and to understand the impact of the revenue you need to go deeper than a ten-word answer. As previously discussed, details about an organization's revenue need to be mined so that revenue KPIs can be created, including: number of new customers, number of existing customers, average transaction size for new and existing customers, average gross margin contribution for new and existing customers, number of orders in a set time period, for new versus existing customers.

This "set of eight" form the bare minimum a business should know about the revenue its customers are providing. The breakdowns of course can get incredibly detailed in various customer segments and product lines; the detail required depends on the business. If, for example, a business has three main product lines, then the breakdown by product line using the set of eight metrics for each should be reviewed. While this task may seem daunting, a calculation may not be required for every reporting period, as generally these metrics move slower and are less fluid than other metrics, unless concentrated effort is applied. Making this process even simpler, many financial systems can be set up to produce automated reports.

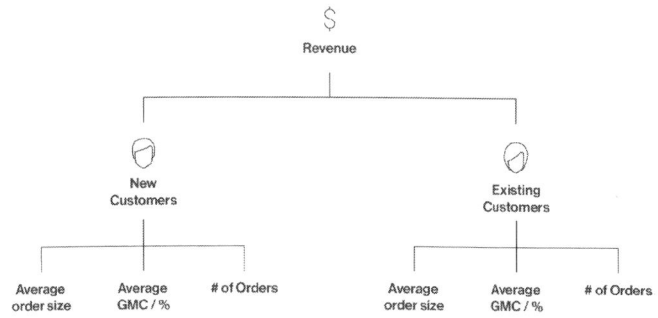

Download this graphic and more at stevewhittington.com

What does this tell us? Gathering this data can help us understand where the business is going very quickly. Let's review the set of eight individually:

Step 1

The first step to gather the data for the set of eight is to segregate your customers using a basic differentiation: New and Existing. For this example, during time period t, company X had 100 customers of which there were:

- 80 New Customers
- 20 Existing Customers

What does this break down tell us? To be fair, it depends

on the business, its stage of maturity, and its goals. If this is a new business and the goal is to acquire customers, this is a basic indicator that the company is headed in the right direction. If this is a mature business with a static revenue stream, this ratio might be worrisome. A business in this scenario is on a treadmill of constantly needing to acquire new customers and only has a retention rate of 20%. If this trend holds month after month, this business clearly needs to focus on retention.

Now that the customers are divided, we can review the revenue metrics between the two groups.

Step 2

The second step is to review the average transaction size (ATS) for new and existing customers.

Average Transaction Size (ATS): The average transaction size is the average sale of a specific cohort over a specific time period. The cohort could include a product grouping, location, department, customers, or individual salesperson.

- New ATS = $1,000
- Existing ATS = $2,500

What does this tell us? It shows the revenue volume by group. With this completed, you will now know what percentage of sales each group represents. It also shows which group spends more. In the example above, repeat buyers clearly spend more. Why? To gain a deeper insight, the *why* needs to be determined; it could be the existing customer trusts the organization more, or this is a result of an upgrade to a more expensive model several years later. If the *why* can be determined, the size of the opportunity for the business to grow and nurture its existing customers to make the purchase can be calculated.

Step 3

The third step is to review gross margin contribution (GMC) and percentage for new and existing customers.

The GMC is a derivative of the average transaction size and margin. So if the AVT grows over time, the GMC will grow as well. The second part of the GMC calculation is the margin; monitoring the results, there are two scenarios that generally happen:

- The new GM is lower than existing, perhaps because to close the first sale the organization offers discounts.

- The old GM is lower, perhaps because accounts become less profitable as the account grows and the buyer demands more concessions.

These scenarios need to be watched and monitored, and the gross margin trends need to be reviewed, as ultimately the gross margin is one of the three basic levers that a business influences to affect the bottom line.

While I have provided "possible" scenarios as to why the GM might be lower, you will need to investigate trends within your business and determine the causes behind the numbers so you can understand what needs to be done.

Step 4

The last step for reviewing revenue metrics is to review the number of orders or transactions for new and existing customers.

Using the starting example of 100 customers during the time period t, how many transactions involved these 100 customers? If there were 200, who made them?

- 80 new customers = 80 transactions
- 20 existing customers = 120 transactions

So what does this tell us? In this scenario, though the loyal customers are a small portion of the overall customers, they are very frequent. Again, the numbers for each business will depend on the business and even seasonal product cycles. Seeking to understand these numbers in order to influence them is the key.

Why is this important? This "set of eight" reveals so much more than just top line revenue. Top line revenue can only be described in two ways, either up or down, and neither label explains what is happening in your business. Organizations work primarily to influence their business using marketing dollars and efforts. There are three buckets of marketing strategy to pour dollars and efforts into: customer acquisition, customer retention, and customer upsell and cross sell. Knowing the "set of eight" revenue KPIs tells you where to spend your marketing dollars. If you have a high ratio of existing customers, you may wish to employ acquisition marketing to grow your customer base. If your average transaction size is low for existing customers, you may wish to add dollars and effort into the cross sell and upsell bucket. If you have very few existing customers, retention and loyalty may be critical marketing allocations. These are just three focused actions that are possible because of the deeper understanding provided by calculating these revenue metrics.

Lastly, now that you know the average transaction size and close rate, you will be able to fully calculate your marketing ROI.

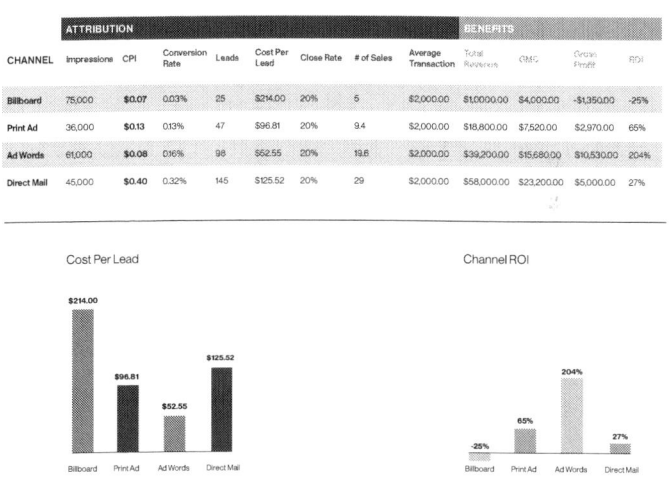

| CHANNEL | ATTRIBUTION | | | | | | | BENEFITS | | | | |
	Impressions	CPI	Conversion Rate	Leads	Cost Per Lead	Close Rate	# of Sales	Average Transaction	Total Revenue	GMS	Gross Profit	ROI
Billboard	75,000	$0.07	0.03%	25	$214.00	20%	5	$2,000.00	$10,000.00	$4,000.00	-$1,350.00	-25%
Print Ad	36,000	$0.13	0.13%	47	$96.81	20%	9.4	$2,000.00	$18,800.00	$7,520.00	$2,970.00	65%
Ad Words	61,000	$0.08	0.16%	98	$52.55	20%	19.6	$2,000.00	$39,200.00	$15,680.00	$10,530.00	204%
Direct Mail	45,000	$0.40	0.32%	145	$125.52	20%	29	$2,000.00	$58,000.00	$23,200.00	$5,000.00	27%

Cost Per Lead

Channel ROI

Download this graphic and more at stevewhittington.com

With full Awareness/Consideration and sale stages gathered, a complete analysis can begin. Consider how a media buy for the billboard channel might have unfolded. In the beginning, the channel appeared to be the best buy based on what was known, cost per impression, but as results were gathered, this channel was clarified as a losing expenditure.

Of note for this example: an overall transaction size was used for the company. For the most part, considering the channels employed, this was primarily acquisition marketing. This format can be easily applied to a retention campaign, and all the numbers can again be specific to that campaign.

Stage 2
SUMMARY AND REFLECTIONS

SUMMARY

REFERRING TO THE last table, one could be tempted to conclude this is all just marketing math. For the most part it is. It is understanding the impact of the qualitative results on your customer journey that matters. As a leader, you need to look deeper than the numbers to understand the story behind them. Overlay the numeric results with a customer journey map to further understand the close rate. Is your sales team capturing and advancing all the leads? Are they applying key account management to existing accounts to grow the revenue? Why is there a difference in the average transaction size between new and existing customers? There are so many possibilities to explore. The math creates a baseline from which to gain understanding.

REFLECTIONS/ACTION ITEMS

- What is your organization's close rate? Can it be improved by 1–2%?

- What are you currently doing to increase your organization's close rate? Can your process be improved with sales team product knowledge, sales training, and sales coaching? What can you start on immediately? Refer to your reflection from Section One, Stage 2.

- How do you review your revenue? What is your average transaction size for existing versus new customers, for your product or service offerings?

- Record your average transaction size and close rate in the worksheet. Calculate your ROI per channel.

- Does the ROI change your perception of the different advertising/promotional channels you are using?

Stage 3
AFTER SALE PROCESS

THE CUSTOMER EXPERIENCE is only beginning when you collect the cheque. The first two stages are how you get a customer; the last two stages are how you keep a customer and turn them into a loyal advocate for your business. While the ability of an organization to deal with the customer after the sale is as important as leading up to the sale, sadly it is often neglected. These processes include customer satisfaction follow up, product training, warranty and ongoing service requirements. They are measured through reviews and the Net Promoter Score.

KPI #6: Reputation Management Ratings

Online reviews are no longer new, they are a fact of life. Consider the impact of the following statistics:

- **93% of consumers say reviews impact purchase decisions.**
- **72% say positive reviews create trust.**
- **A negative review may drive away up to 22% of customers.**

Source: MarketingLand

Online reviews are often mismanaged or left at a distance and sometimes ignored. The main review online platforms for many businesses include Facebook, Google, and Yelp, plus overall social listening. However, there are industry specific review platforms such as TripAdvisor, Homestars for renovation contractors, and reviews of various employers can be found on Glassdoor or Ratemyemployer.ca. As an organization, at a minimum, you need to have all your locations independently set up with a Google my Business page and of course have a presence on Facebook. While capturing and managing reviews on social media is important, social media is also a customer service channel for answering questions, inquiries, and complaints, so make sure your channels are monitored and measured.

BEST PRACTICE

DEALING WITH BAD REVIEWS

Bad reviews are going to happen. We do not live in a world in which everything is five-star or 10 out of 10. The question most businesses obsessively worry about is what to do when a bad review happens (it will, so don't think the sky is falling when it happens!).

Step 1

For your peace of mind, understand that a bad review

does not make yours a bad business. In fact, consumers will be suspicious if you do not have one or two bad reviews.

Step 2

Acknowledge and engage with the customer publicly online and offer to create a solution by providing direct access to a decision maker offline. Follow a consistent communication process when you respond. Customer service professionals commonly employ a four-step protocol:

1. Thank the customer for the review.

2. Apologize and empathize.

3. Work towards a solution.

4. Take the communication offline.

Example

Review:

⋆⋆ out of 5: "I was very disappointed with the product I purchased at your location and felt when I called to get some clarification on why a part did not fit I was dismissed by staff and offered no solution." -Emma

Response:

"Hi, Emma. Thank you for bringing this interaction to our attention. (**Step 1**) I can only imagine your frustration with getting your purchase home and then not having it fit together, combined with the lack of support you received when you called. I sincerely apologize for this experience. (**Step 2**) This is not how we desire for our customers to be treated and goes against our values. Our store manager Kristie has been made aware of your circumstances, and would like to make things right. (**Step 3**) Her direct line is XXX-XXX-XXXX. (**Step 4**) Her request to you is to give us another opportunity to make things right. On behalf of company XYZ, again, I sincerely apologize."

This interaction shows both Emma and the world that you care, while also providing an opportunity to take the potential messiness of the situation out of the public domain to where it can be handled privately. Any customer reading this review can tell that the company cares and acknowledges their mistakes, and that they will attempt to resolve the problem. Businesses are made up of people, and people make mistakes. Your customers are people and generally are accepting that people (like them) make mistakes. What often matters most is not that the mistake happened, but acknowledgment of the mistake.

Step 3

Turning a 1 star review into a 10 out of 10.

As an organization, you can look at every bad review as a gift. Once the handling of the review has been taken offline, you have the chance to fix a problem and turn a detractor into a promoter by using your service recovery process. It has been my experience that when you address bad reviews quickly and genuinely—and solve the problem—you have a customer for life. To date in my career, there has not been a single customer whose bad review, when handled properly with a recovery process, has not gone down this path. At the Flaman Group of Companies, every bad review is brought to the attention of a key executive. That is how seriously customer satisfaction is taken; the customers know this and respect the attention provided when things go wrong. Beyond executive attention, the bad reviews are showcased across the organization as learning opportunities of what not to do and how to be proactive. The two actions together (executive attention and using every opportunity to learn) reinforce a culture of customer centricity.

What does this tell us? Reviews and messages are *the voice of the customer*. Ratings tell a brand how they are doing, often with explanations. This is a clear indicator of how an organization's staff or its process treats its customers.

INSIGHT

VOICE OF THE CUSTOMER

The voice of the customer (or VOC) is generally defined as an in-depth marketing research technique used to understand customer needs and wants, and provides an opportunity for the business to prioritize needs and wants based on a customer-defined importance.

Reputation management ratings provide insight into the level of satisfaction of your customers. A 3 out of 5 would, as an aggregate rating, indicate that an organization is average. But like all numerical results, the understanding is not in the tallied result, but how the result got tallied.

Comments and reviews, considered individually, can provide a greater degree of understanding. If 50% of your reviews were 1 and 50% were 5 you would receive a 3, but clearly your organization is not average. Your organization is exceptional half the time and horrible the other half. This could immediately point to lack of process, or the need for further training.

Having a review gathering processes in place to capture elements of the VOC will give you deeper understanding of your customers' experiences. The reason an organization collects and reviews this data is because generally you don't know when things are bad or good. Thus, you don't know what you don't know and most customers, when they have a bad experience, just go away; of those who have an amazing experience, very few volunteer that information.

The point is, good or bad (but more likely for bad), very few customers will share feedback. This is why you need to build a process to ask for feedback to capture the VOC, sending a Net Promoter Score (NPS) survey after every purchase, making sure you are ready and able to receive and respond to reviews on all major platforms, Google, Facebook, Yelp, and then asking for reviews at the completion of every transaction. Only by earnestly asking for feedback will you receive it and thus have the opportunity to respond, understand, learn (from the good and bad), and improve.

Why is this important? Through reviews, a brand can conduct service recovery for the world to see. How a brand reacts to good or bad reviews helps or detracts from future business. As such, **all reviews (good, average and bad)**

need to be answered so that customers see that a brand is paying attention. **Bad reviews, if embraced, present an opportunity for the brand to improve**. The reviews also provide empirical evidence to company staff and thus can be a marker to gauge progress.

An interesting exercise can be done to help improve performance. In the first episode of Reid Hoffman's podcast *Masters of Scale,* the guest Brian Chesky, Co-founder of Airbnb, described how they created exceptional experiences at scale with the Airbnb platform. It began by brainstorming about what certain ratings on a scale from 1 out of 5, to 2, to 3, and so on, would look like, and how customers would react. Once they got to 5 out 5, they then brainstormed what 6 out of 5, might look like, and then 7 out of 5, and 8 and 9, and so on. The point of the exercise was two-fold: to define what is needed to be done to achieve higher ratings, and to change mindsets. Once 10 out of 5 was defined, a 5 or 6 out of 5 did not look nearly as difficult. The team then went to work training its staff and its hosts on what to do in order to get higher ratings. In the business of being a host, having a high rating is the only method you have for getting business, as is becoming true for all businesses.

KPI # 7: Net Promoter Score (NPS)

The Net Promoter Score has been labeled by some as the most important metric a business can measure. The Net Promoter Score is the one metric that will measure how likely your customers are to recommend your business, products, and services. If all your customers were wowed by your customer experience, you would not need marketing;

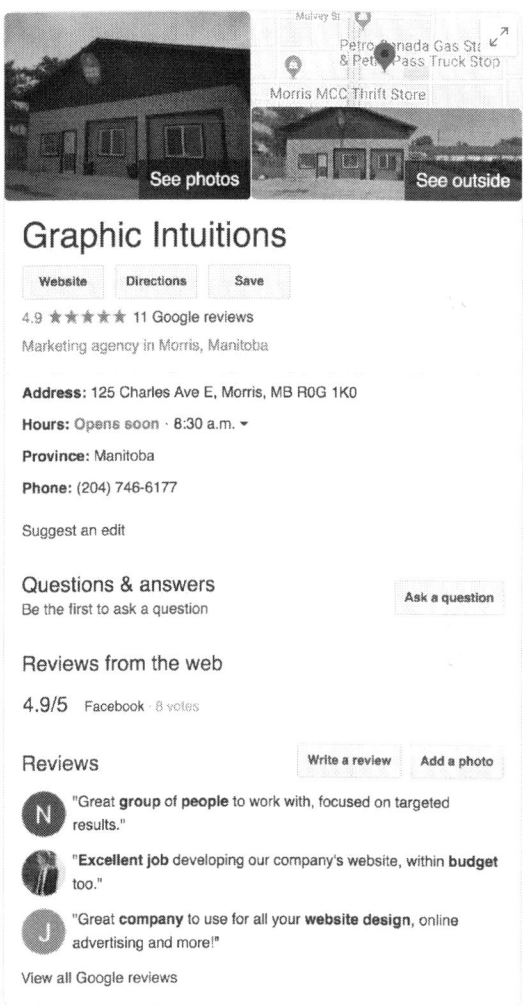

Graphic Intuitions

| Website | Directions | Save |

4.9 ★★★★★ 11 Google reviews

Marketing agency in Morris, Manitoba

Address: 125 Charles Ave E, Morris, MB R0G 1K0

Hours: Opens soon · 8:30 a.m. ▾

Province: Manitoba

Phone: (204) 746-6177

Suggest an edit

Questions & answers
Be the first to ask a question

| Ask a question |

Reviews from the web

4.9/5   Facebook · 8 votes

Reviews

| Write a review | Add a photo |

"Great **group** of **people** to work with, focused on targeted results."

"**Excellent job** developing our company's website, within **budget** too."

"Great **company** to use for all your **website design**, online advertising and more!"

View all Google reviews

Download this graphic and more at stevewhittington.com

your business would be built on referrals. As previously mentioned, advertising can be considered a tax you pay. In the case of the NPS, and as famously quoted by Robert Stephens **"Advertising in the tax you pay for being unremarkable"**.

What does this tell us? The Net Promoter Score is calculated by taking the percentage of your promoters minus your detractors. The higher the score, the higher your likelihood of repeat business and referrals. Moreover, inconsistencies in your score over time point to other challenges in your organization. Large fluctuations between time periods, territories, or even as granular as a per sales person can help focus organizational training efforts.

NPS Dashboard

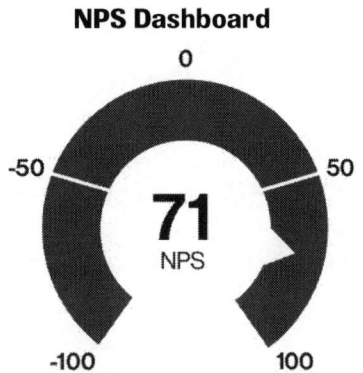

Download this graphic and more at stevewhittington.com

Why is this important? With higher repeat business and referrals, compounding effects occur. First, you will be able to increase the lifetime value (see appendix for formula) of your customer base. By keeping your customer base loyal, to grow your business, you simply keep marketing to add more customers if the market size can allow for this. This customer base growth will occur easily with a high Net Promoter Score and thus referrals.

BEST PRACTICE

NET PROMOTER SCORE AND WHY YOU NEED IT

Imagine a world in which your customers are so excited after shopping at your organization that they rush out to tell their friends and family. If this happened with every one of your customers, you wouldn't need to spend a dollar on advertising because all your advertising would be done for you. (Yes, this is a bit of an exaggeration—but you get the point!)

Sales would skyrocket; earnings would double; staff, stakeholders, and obviously customers would all be happier. This is not a fantasy world; this can be achieved by managing a rating by customers from one simple question: "How likely are you to recommend?" This is called the Net Promoter Score.

> "This metric creates a simple scorecard for the organization that has been shown by Bain & Company research, as well as research by a growing number of unaffiliated experts and executives, to explain significant variations in revenue growth rates among companies in head-to-head competition. In Bain & Company research, differences in the relative competitive Net Promoter Scores explain anywhere from 10%

> to 70% of the variation in subsequent revenue growth rates among direct competitors. The Net Promoter® leader in a market grows, on average, more than two times faster than its competitors in that market."
>
> -Bain and Company

The Net Promoter System is a system that generates a rating to gauge customer loyalty. It is blindingly simple: it is based on the rating that a customer gives when asked the question "How likely are you to recommend?" Customers are then categorized into three groups: promoters, passives, and detractors. The score is simply the percentage of promoters minus the percentage of detractors.

NPS Scale

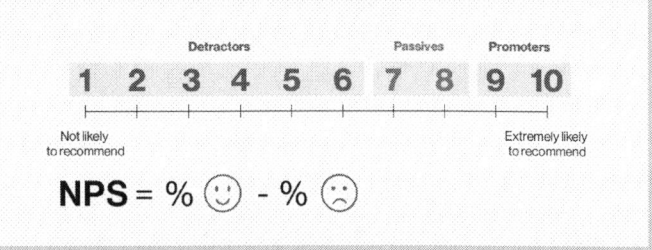

Download this graphic and more at stevewhittington.com

So you have a number? Now what?

What gets measured, get managed; what gets managed well, gets improved. By having an objective number and system in place to capture customer feedback, you now know how you are doing, and you can measure objective improvement moving forward. Most organizations want to improve and grow. While sales and earnings are the ultimate measure of growth, having a high NPS has been proven to accelerate growth.

Lastly, as the NPS system is gaining in popularity, it is very easy to benchmark your business against your industry. Benchmarking will help you establish what a bad, good, or great score is in relation to your industry. Keep in mind that the first time you benchmark can either be a delightful surprise or a dreadful surprise depending how you land compared to your peers.

Stage 3
SUMMARY AND REFLECTIONS

SUMMARY

MEASURING YOUR AFTER sale experience is critical for your business success. Most customers experience buyers' remorse not because of what they bought, but what they experience after the purchase. As an organization leader, you must understand what is happening; the only way to do that is through surveys and review ratings. While the net promoter is often proclaimed as the ultimate customer or client satisfaction indicator, it may not provide insights into a specific problem area. Often once managers begin to receive data insights on their customers, they want more. If you are new to conducting surveys and listening to the voice of your customer, start with the NPS and online reputation management. Master these elements first, before beginning to develop more complex customer satisfaction surveys.

As you start measuring and improving your customer journey, be mindful of the cost of a 10 out of 10. Before you improve upon your customer experience to an exceptional

level, most of your 10 out of 10 reviews will be a result of an unsustainable action. Let me explain: In the beginning of your improvement journey, most cases of a 10 out of 10 result from a brand responding to and fixing a previous bad experience. Often, in a reaction to fix the situation and get the customer turned into a promoter, cost considerations are removed, and the brand goes overboard to make things right. In most cases, these 10 out of 10 ratings lose the organization money.

If you go through the exercise of defining what each rating point looks like for your business aim for 9 out of 10 every time. That is typically sustainable, and you are likely to pick up true 10 ratings along the way.

REFLECTIONS/ACTION ITEMS

- What is your organization's NPS? Do you conduct NPS surveys?

- If you conduct NPS surveys, are they aggregate or granular for your organization? What would be the benefit in either case?

- Is responding to reviews part of your service recovery process?

- Do you respond to all reviews (both good and bad)?

- If you want to "bake in" customer satisfaction to your team, one tactic has been tying the NPS score to performance bonuses. Your people create your customer journey, perhaps an incentive will go a long way towards achieving that goal.

- Brainstorm about your ratings: What would it take and how would the customer feel for each rating point? What does a 1 out of 5? 2? 3? 4? 5? even 6 out of 5 look like for your business?

Stage 4
RETENTION AND REFERRAL

ONE OF THE three main categories of marketing is customer retention or loyalty marketing. It is in Stage 4 of the customer journey that a brand applies loyalty marketing. There are many ways to do this, but it typically involves creating ongoing touches to ensure that the customer's needs are looked after quickly and fairly after a sale or service, and that future needs are anticipated and considered. The brand needs to legitimately care about their customers, which is accomplished using authentic individualized ongoing communications for B2C and key account management for B2B.

The metric for measuring your efforts at retaining customers is a simple one: customer churn.

Beyond measuring a metric, this stage is also about leveraging the customer advocates you already have. The measurement will allow you to target those customers. Who better to ask for leads than customers that love what you do? According to HubSpot, after a positive experience, **83% of customers would be happy to provide a referral**. But salespeople aren't asking—just 29% of customers end up *giving* a referral. On average, up to 65% of your happy customers are not being leveraged for referrals. I suspect for most businesses that represents a huge opportunity.

KPI #8: Customer Churn

Customer churn is the quantity of customers over a given time period that are not repeat customers. It measures the amount of customers that an organization loses. For instance, if you had 100 customers at time t and during the next period, time t+1, you had 80 of those customers conduct repeat business with you, your churn is 20%: 100 – 80 = 20 lost customers; 20/100 = 20%.

What does this tell us? Customer churn educates a brand on their retention rate or repeat business rate. It provides guidance for where an organization should be placing marketing dollars to help grow the business. It also identifies who the good customers are and who the brand is failing.

Why is this important? If an organization knows its churn rate, it can use this metric to focus efforts based on the nature of its industry. If there is a high lifetime value of a customer, retaining customers is a critical battle for a brand. If customers can be continually acquired and retained at a higher rate, that equals a recipe for growth. Loyal customers can be leveraged for referrals and also targeted with marketing or key account management to ensure you keep them. Note that the customer you've lost can be targeted for future acquisition campaigns and surveys to learn what went wrong.

Stage 4
SUMMARY AND REFLECTIONS

SUMMARY

KNOWING YOUR CHURN rate is a critical health indicator of your business. If no customers are returning (or very few), you will be stuck on the acquisition treadmill, going nowhere, before eventually getting too tired of running—and then falling off.

REFLECTIONS/ACTION ITEMS

- What is a reasonable time period for repeat purchases in your business?

- Calculate your churn rate.

- Do you ask for referrals? If not, make it part of your sale process.

BRINGING IT ALL TOGETHER: MOVING THE NEEDLE FOR YOUR BUSINESS

Business is a good game—lots of competition and a minimum of rules. You keep score with money.

-Nolan Bushnell,

Founder of Atari and Chuck E. Cheese's

IN THE NEXT section, you will be shown how to start learning about your organization's customer journey through mapping and creating a baseline of measurement. It is this baseline data that will allow you to understand what is happening in your business and where the opportunities are. The eight metrics showcased in this section are the baseline and the framework that can be used to move the financial results of the business.

1. Total Advertising Reach

2. Conversion Rate

3. Lead Count

4. Close Rate

5. Revenue Metrics

6. Reputation Management

7. Net Promoter Score

8. Churn Rate

To showcase how this framework can be applied, sample metrics have been created for a fictitious retailer. The metrics are being applied at an overall aggregate level. In practice, this framework can be applied to any level of detail you require for your business. These levels could be by division or store or customer segment, or by an individual journey.

Example

You are the owner of a single store furniture retailer. You desire to grow the business and you know the following metrics for the previous 12-month time period (t).

Reach:	5,000,000 impressions
Conversion Rate:	1.3%
Leads:	65,000
Close Rate:	15%
Revenue:	$12,187,500
Average Transaction Size:	$1,250
Customers:	9,750
Reputation Rating:	3.5 out of 5

NPS:	41
Churn:	70%

Given the above figures, what could you do? What would you do?

Looking at these number there are three quick areas that could be worked on which would have immediate impact:

1. You could grow the business without any more leads by increasing the close rate.

2. The conversion rate of marketing could be improved to acquire more leads.

3. You could pay for more advertising to increase your reach.

4. Beyond these three items, customer retention could be improved, which will help the next period.

Given all the options, let's examine the effect of just one change.

What would the above business look like with an **increased conversion rate from 1.3% to 1.6%?**

The Codifying Formula

	CURRENT	INCREASING CONVERSION RATE
Reach	5,000,000	5,000,000
Conversion Rate	1.30%	1.60%
Leads	65,000	80,000
Close Rate	15%	15%
Revenue	$12,187,500.00	$15,000,000.00
Average Transaction	1,250	1,250
Customer	9,750	12,000
Reputation Rating	3.5 out of 5	3.5 out of 5
NPS	41	41
Churn	70%	70%

A simple increase in the conversion on your ads **would increase revenue by $2,812,500.**

Perhaps the offers and ads are as good as they can get for this organization, and increasing the advertising effectiveness is not an option. If external factors cannot be influenced, it is always a good practice to look internally to see what you can do with what you have.

Given this scenario, with sales and service training, perhaps you could quickly increase the close rate by 3% and reduce churn by 5%, leaving everything else as is. By doing this, you would immediately gain 1,950 customers through the sale process, and keep 487 more customers via retention and referrals.

The Codifying Formula

	CURRENT	INCREASE CLOSE REDUCE CHURN
Reach	5,000,000	5,000,000
Conversion Rate	1.30%	1.30%
Leads	65,000	65,000
Close Rate	15%	18%
Revenue	$12,187,500.00	$14,625,000.00
Average Transaction	1,250	1,250
Customer	9,750	11,700
Reputation Rating	3.5 out of 5	3.5 out of 5
NPS	41	41
Churn	70%	65%

*note effect of reduced Churn would show up in the next recording period

Once again, there is an increase in revenue in this period of $2,437,500.00. However, with the reduced churn there will be a further effect on revenues for the next period.

Net Retained Customers (Customers × Churn Reduction) × Average Transaction Rate = Net Increased Revenue from reduced churn

Retained Customers (11,700 × (70–65%)) × $1250 = $731,250 Increased Revenue in the next period

**This example considers that your returning customers have the same average transaction size as new customers; often this in not the case, which is why it is important in your revenue metrics to understand the average transaction size between new and existing (retained) customers.

In this scenario, small tweaks to two metrics equalled over $3.1 M in increased revenues for the next time period.

One way of deciding which metric to focus on is to understand the different effect each metric will have:

- The first four metrics (Reach, Conversion Rate, Leads, Close Rate) will have an immediate effect on revenue.

- The last four (Average Transaction Size, Reputation Management, NPS, Churn) take longer to make a change, and generally do not have an immediate effect (except for churn if the purchase cycles are rapid and reoccurring) and require an improvement to the overall experience your customer has.

Long-term initiatives related to customer service training and retention processes will reduce churn and increase your reputation rating, which will lead to a higher NPS, which will then lead to more customers returning and being acquired through word-of-mouth.

If you can maintain your customer acquisition pace and increase your customer retention and saturation, with the first four metrics and last four metrics working in tandem, you will quickly grow your business.

All the data points are connected. The customer journey is not a linear line—it is wheel that goes around and around, and along the way you can tweak stages and measure outcomes to gauge improvement. By doing so, you can create breakthrough growth. What gets measured gets managed, and if it is measured using this framework, it gets optimized.

To truly utilize the numbers within this framework and learn how to improve them, an organization will need thorough customer understanding. However, a deep understanding of an organization's customers can only be achieved by mapping customer journeys using these critical metrics (moments of truth).

Section Three
STARTING YOUR CUSTOMER EXPERIENCE TRANSFORMATION

The T-Mobile model is paying huge dividends for the company: In three years since launch, T-Mobile's overall cost to serve is down 13%, its Net Promoter Score (a measure of customer loyalty) is up by more than half, and its customer churn rate has dipped to an all-time low.

-Harvard Business Review,

November—December 2018.

CLEARLY T-MOBILE EMBARKED on a campaign to change its customer experience, recognizing that this is the most important driver of business, and is now measuring the outcomes using key metrics. To achieve this goal, they had to change the culture of their customer service team. In fact, they completely changed the way their teams worked and focused on a simple goal: Customer Happiness.

In his book *Fundamentally Different*, David Friedman argues that culture is the foundation of organizational success, and defining and measuring critical behaviours is the way to manage culture. I completely agree. To start a customer journey transformation, an organization must be prepared to alter its culture, as T-Mobile did. As stated in Section Two, most organizations believe they are delivering excellent customer service, though the customers may believe otherwise. The only way to change this outcome will be by altering behaviours. The only way to improve the behaviours of your team will be by measuring the results of behaviors and presenting the objective truth as a learning tool.

To initiate your organization's customer experience transformation, you must be prepared to obsessively measure the outcomes of behaviours that define your customer journey. Creating objective data around all actions (or moments of truth) is a radical shift for most organizations.

The first place to start is to determine where you are today. What is your current customer experience? Why are the outcomes what they are? While doing this, be prepared to assess your current culture and understand that in order to improve, you will need to shift from where you are today to a newly defined customer-centric culture.

To create this new culture of measurement and learning about your customer journey, you will need to follow some basic steps:

Step 1: Map your existing customer journey

Document all the paths customers take with your organization, and define every step of their journey.

Step 2: Mine your data and create a baseline for interpretation

Determine the data you currently have, identify any gaps in the data, it's clean up, and segmentation as required. This will provide you with a starting point to fill in your new framework.

Step 3: Set goals and measure against them

Create a regular reporting rhythm with goals to measure against. This will enable you to interpret the data and create actionable insights.

Step 4: Create target market profiles

Now that you have data to help you to understand your customers, the next step is to create full profiles on your customers. Having a detailed understanding of your customers is a precursor for the next step.

Step 5: Design your customer journey

At this point, you have learned what is working and what is not working with regards to your current customer journeys, and you have developed a deeper understanding of your customers. With your teams, you are now ready to start designing new customer journeys.

Step 6: Implement

Create a communication plan for the culture shift and your new customer journeys, and then implement.

Step 7: Measure the results and iterate

Determine if further improvements can be made. Then, pick another path and design a new journey. Repeat these steps as needed.

Step 8: Communicate the results—Create a data democracy

Create a dashboard for all to see. Share the metrics that matter so that all team members can understand, engage, and learn from the process.

Through the systematic implementation of these steps, you will begin your own customer journey improvement path. Be warned! This is a journey that never ends; in essence it is a mountain with no top! However, it will create a culture of continuous improvement for your customer experience, which will create two winners: your organization and your customers.

Step 1
MAP YOUR EXISTING CUSTOMER JOURNEY

TO UNDERSTAND WHERE you need to go, you need to begin by clearly defining where you are.

Any student of lean or process improvement will state that the first step to improving a process is to document the current state, with the understanding that if work is getting done there is a process in place, even if it is not written down. The customer experience an organization provides is a derivative of its processes and how those process are executed by people and technology to create an entire customer journey.

Definition of customer journey: **all the interactions or touchpoints a customer has with an organization before, during and after the purchase and/or service experience**. This process starts with the first awareness of need for a product or service, and moves through the completion of the transaction and after service elements.

To start your mapping, you will need to do a considerable

amount of prep work. One exercise to help understand your current customer journey is to answer questions related to your brand regarding the 7 Ps of modern marketing. The 7 Ps are:

1. **Product:** What is your product? What is the product mix? How is your product used and what are the warranties?

2. **Promotion:** What marketing communication is used? Advertising, sales promotion, direct marketing, public relations, branding?

3. **Price:** What is your price positioning? Are there discounts? Credit terms, payment methods, free or value-added inclusions?

4. **Place:** What are the trade channels you sell through, and the supports for each channel? Are there segments?

5. **People:** Who are your customer-facing people? What is their training? What is your culture?

6. **Process:** What processes do you have documented? Are they business led, customer-focused led or IT led?

7. **Physical evidence:** What is the contact experience with your sales/customer-facing staff? What is the online experience, the physical store experience, the lot experience, the delivery experience, the after sale experience, and the support experience?

As you start to answer these questions, you may find there are different experiences based on product, customer segments, or channels. This exercise will bring to light the paths you will need to define or further refine. Also, it will begin to highlight all the various and potential touchpoints your organization has with the customer.

So how do you map a customer journey? Considering that you have now answered the seven P's, most likely you have come across organizational documents on existing processes, customer personas, and you have an idea of the scope of your various customer journeys and the limitations these journeys face in the current state. The next step in your preparation is to gather all this information; you will then have quite a few pieces of the puzzle. For instance, you should have your sale process, delivery process, warranty process, buyer's journey and/or nurturing campaigns, all of which map out large pieces of your customer journey.

After gathering up all available information it is now time to gather a cross-functional team. If you are a student of business process management, you will be familiar with the concept of swim lanes for process maps. Swim Lane Process Maps, as defined by The Business Process Management Common Body of Knowledge, merely incorporate simple flow charts—generally represented as long vertical lines resembling the channel or lane markings in swimming competitions. These lines help arrange the flow of activities or tasks by function area, making it easy to visualize handoffs in work.

Simple 30,000 ft view swim lane diagram of a marketing campaign.

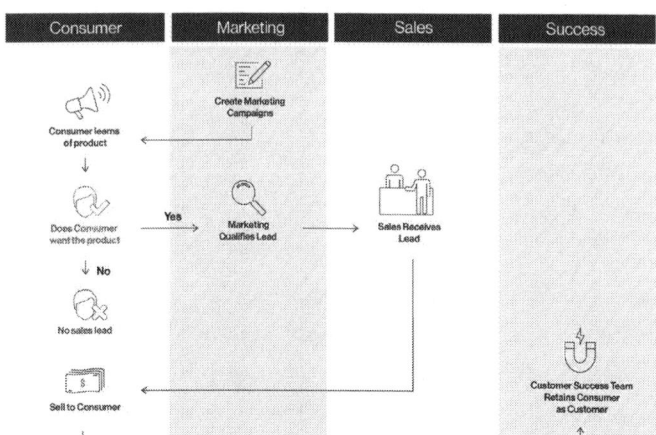

Download this graphic and more at stevewhittington.com

The process I propose for customer journey mapping utilizes swim lane process mapping for each customer touchpoint. With all these organizational assets in place, it is now finally time to roll up your sleeves and get to work brainstorming touchpoints and who is involved.

Consider the purchase of lumber from a lumber yard. Think of all the touchpoints that organization has for a customer to complete a purchase. For each touchpoint what functions might be involved? At the beginning it could be marketing, and then sales, and then yard staff, and then customer service. In this case, you would gather representatives from each of these function areas to ask their input to map out your current customer journey.

There are many ways to map customer journeys. Some are

very simple, basically just writing out all the touchpoints with a customer in a linear diagram. Others are more detailed, using swim lanes, flow charts and artists to create graphical representations. In all cases brainstorming is involved, a blank white wall, sticky notes and willingness to authentically examine the organizations processes to map current state customer journey touchpoints.

A great way to brain storm is to use the four stages of the customer journey as headings and then using an individual sticky note for each touchpoint, document all the touchpoints your organization has grouping the sticky notes under each stage. When it comes time to map a market segment you should have all the touchpoints documented to choose from.

The template I propose to use can be downloaded from www.stevewhittington.com and requires preparation and a deep understanding about your customer to fully complete. It forces you to take your brainstormed touchpoints and think about the journey from two contexts, the customer and your internal processes, while aligning a KPI for measurement. These critical contexts must always be present when you are mapping: **Outside in (the customer experience of the journey) and Inside out (your employee experience of the journey).** Both sides of the customer journey need to be improved to create a sustainable increase in effectiveness and satisfaction.

If you are just starting out, more than likely you will not have everything you need because you have not been measuring the data, nor will you have complete target market profiles. Do not lose sleep about not having all the pieces at this point. It is expected that you will not have them in place. Using the template provided with your cross-functional team gathered and the prep work you completed, start filling in the blanks.

While the steps to take are simple, the work is not. Summarizing the steps for customer journey mapping is as follows:

1. Record your findings from working through the seven P's of marketing.

2. Gather all available organizational assets that document your customers and your processes with your customers.

3. Gather your cross-functional team and brainstorm all touchpoints for your overall customer journey.

4. Pick the first market segment to map (refer to the target market profiles step later in this section for details on how to define market segments).

5. Utilize the Customer Journey Mapping worksheet to populate the selected market segment from the two contexts (Outside in, and Inside out). Be sure to stick to current state and do not begin designing. You need to fully understand the current state to provide insights for future improved designed journeys.

6. Once you have documented your map with all the touchpoints by stage and aligned KPI's, it is now time to validate the map with your customer. Reach out to customers you can trust to ask if the

experience you have mapped for them (the customer process in relation to your touchpoints) is in fact what they experience. To start, focus on the touchpoints that matter (the moments of truth) instead of the whole map. To receive quick validation, email surveys or phone calls may be all you need to receive the feed back required to validate or cause a rework on parts of your map.

Admittedly, though this is only a six-step process, there is considerable work involved in order to execute the steps. However, it is always an exciting and illuminating process to truly learn what your customer journey is. I have never had a team conduct a mapping exercise for the "as is" process and not be surprised by the number of steps involved, or the path, customer and employee effort required.

Sample Customer Journey Map

PRODUCT/SERVICE: ROLL OFF DUMP TRAILER
GOALS: CURRENT STATE BASELINE
TARGET MARKET PROFILE: CONSTRUCTION CAZ

STAGES	AWARENESS/CONSIDERATION				SALE PROCESS			
Touch Point	Social Post	PPC Ad	Landing Page	Web inquiry	Sales Response	Product Demo	Quote	Finance/ Purchase
Customer Process	Social browsing interacts with post	Internet Search, click on ad	Review Landing Page	Send in inquiry	Receive response decide to learn more	Come to store to Review product	Request a quote	Make payment arrangements
Internal Process	Marketing builds post	Marketing builds ads	Marketing builds web pages with sales offer	Marketing reviews lead, passes to sales	Sales uses template to respond within 3 hrs of receiving lead	Arrange demo with client, work with technicians to be ready for demo. Demonstrate product using circle feature selling technique	Prepare quote and send to client. Follow up on quote to close deal	Prepare finance documentations and title transfer for registration, fill out internal PDI and delivery forms
Experience: VOC Moments of truth	Passive	Passive	Promoter	Passive	Promoter	Detractor	Passive	Passive
Metric	Reach	Reach	Conversion Rate	Leads			Close Rate	Revenue Metrics
Current State or Goal	8,000	2,560	0.30%	35			20%	AVT = $17,500

STAGES	AFTER SALE PROCESS			RETENTION REFERRAL			
Touch Point	Delivery	Product Training	After Sales Follow up	Product Use	NPS	Warranty	Advocacy
Customer Process	Work with service to arrange a time	Run through of product by rep	Receive Call	Happy with use	Receive email	n/a	Recommend company
Internal Process	PDI unit, arrange delivery time, schedule staff and trucks, load equipment, deliver to customer	Conduct training processes and review warranty documentation	Sales follow up call, 3 days after purchase, conduct follow up questionnaire	n/a	Send NPS survey	n/a	Continual customer touches and follow ups: 30 and 330 days after purchase
Experience: VOC Moments of truth	Promoter	Promoter	Detractor	Promoter	Promoter	Detractor	Promoter
Metric		Reputation Management			NPS		Churn Rate
Current State or Goal		4.2			60		40%

Download this graphic and more at stevewhittington.com

Step 1
SUMMARY AND REFLECTIONS

SUMMARY

CUSTOMER JOURNEY MAPPING can be a complex exercise. One factor is that it depends on how detailed you decide to go with your mapping. For instance, how many touchpoints occur when a customer comes into a store or calls your business? Is the impression the customer has of the physical location a touchpoint that matters to you and your customers? How about reception or a greeter? Every organization will have created a different customer journey, and thus create a different experience. When you decide to map your customer journey, the level of detail should come down to this question: does it affect the customer? Is it a moment of truth that can influence the journey? If so, then the touchpoint should be mapped, and if possible, measured.

REFLECTIONS

- What processes and data do you already have? As a starting point, gather everything.

- Review your 7 Ps, how many customer segments does your organization have? This is a good starting point for understanding how many different customer journeys you will have to map.

- In reviewing your customer journey, think about where pain points are for your customers. Are there common themes with pain points? For instance, do they occur at handoffs from one function to another? These pain points will be a good starting point when you move to designing new journeys (without the pain points).

Step 2
MINE YOUR DATA AND CREATE A BASELINE FOR INTERPRETATION

CUSTOMER-CENTRIC = DATA-CENTRIC. Many companies do not realise the amount of data they have nor what they need to "clean up" so that their data can become usable. This step identifies what an organization has for data, what it needs for data, and how to obtain it; then, what must be done to use the data to create a baseline for improvement. Once you have your journeys mapped with metrics applied, you can begin to review the data and understand where your organization currently stands.

Start by reviewing the data points that you currently have. Do you know your website traffic? Call volume? Leads? What customer data do you have? Many organizations are already measuring some of these critical data points.

Once you understand what you have, you can begin to fill in the gaps and set up tools for gathering the rest. For instance, if you have website traffic but have not captured the data for conversions off your website, that is a good place to start. While this might seem like Marketing 101, it is sometimes surprising that many organizations do not systematically gather and analyze this data. Part of the culture that is now being created is a culture in which gathering and interpreting data about your customer journey is at the forefront of everything you do. If it can't be measured, it should not be done, is an easy rule to live by. Your goal is to measure all eight of the major customer journey KPIs, as explained in the previous section, so you can develop a complete understanding of where you are.

One of the biggest challenges for most organizations when they are starting out is to set up the tools for gathering data and reporting on all the data in one place. Thus, the modern organizational tech stack has developed, it links an organization's marketing automation/lead generation software, CRM (customer relationship management), and ERP (enterprise resource planning software) together to offer a true 360-degree view of an organization's actions and impacts upon their customer journey.

INSIGHT

HOW A TECH STACK WORKS

A broad definition of a tech stack is that it is the technology platforms required to manage your customer and business processes. Historically, these have all been separate systems. A modern tech stack integrates all the elements so that an action in one will create an output or trigger in another. A modern tech stack would include a website that integrates with marketing automation software, your CRM, and your ERP or accounting software.

A typical interaction could go as follows: An order is placed, and in the process a customer account is set up. This automatically relieves inventory from the accounting system, books the revenue, places the customer account information into a customer profile which triggers a thank you email, and begins a tracking campaign to note customer preferences and, in the future, send specific, personalized information on products that the customer has shown interest in. All this of course will be tracked in the CRM, so when an account rep contacts the customer, they are aware of all details of the interactions the customer has had with the company.

While there are common broad elements to most modern tech stacks, such as a website, marketing automation, CRM, and ERP, there are differences in how business processes are mapped and integrated through the tech stack. The integration and digitalization of BPM (Business Process Management) is redefining competitive advantage in today's marketplace.

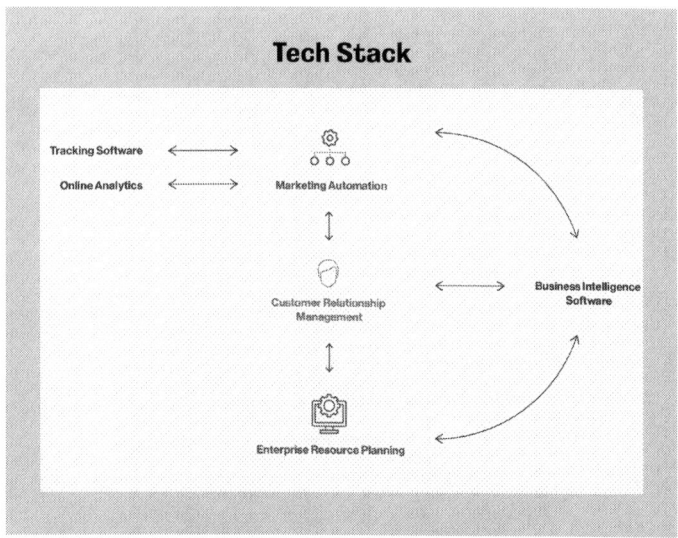

Download this graphic and more at stevewhittington.com

If you do not have the resources to implement a tech stack, don't worry. There are cost effective platforms available that you can use to gather data to create transformational insights for your organization. For each of the eight essential KPIs I've outlined in Section Two, I'll take you through at least one cost effective way you can start to gather or mine the data yourself.

KPI #1: REACH

The total impressions of all your promotion activities over a given time period.

The way to measure reach depends on the channel used, as there are methods to employ to measure each channel. The main channels for promotion activities are: **print, online,**

radio, video, direct marketing, out of home, and events. To measure reach, you need to determine how to quantify the total number of impressions and the total number of unique impressions over a time period on a per channel basis. The dawn of the internet has made this step easier for organizations, as the traditional mediums have all been forced to compete with digital, which can provide to-the-second metrics on impressions, users, click-through rate, conversions, and ultimately revenue through free analytic platforms.

Print

For any print publication you can easily find out the number of copies distributed. You can be conservative and use that number for impressions or, if it is a free publication available in public spaces, you could add a factor for multiple readership. The choice is yours for what you decide to count on a per publication basis, but you will know the number of copies distributed to base your measurement on.

Online

There was a time that online measurement used to be a single platform. Now it depends on the online channels that you use. The way you will measure will come down to three aggregate methods: the online channels you own, the impressions you earn, and the impressions you pay for. So think of your promotion online in these three buckets: owned, earned, and paid.

Owned online channels are basically two platforms, your website and your email list. Both are easy to track. Google analytics is free and you can track the impressions (user sessions) your website receives during time period t very quickly and easily. You simply have to insert a tracking code for the pages on your website you wish to track and then start receiving results. There are entire books and courses dedicated to web analytics, including Google Analytics Academy. The courses are free and certification can be obtained.

Your email impressions can be counted as the number of emails sent that did not bounce back from the sender due to an incorrect email address, as technically the email may be viewed in an inbox even though it is not opened. I, however, only count opened emails. All third party email Software-as-a-Service providers, such as MailChimp, Constant Contact, and Get Response offer a long list of metrics to review, so if you are just starting with the basic metric of impressions, this is easy to gather. Email may also be integrated into your tech stack as part of your marketing automation; if this is the case, reports will be easy to generate.

Earned impressions are from social channels, such as Facebook, LinkedIn, Twitter, Instagram, and Pinterest. In some cases, the analytics in your business accounts actually describe the amount of impressions or users reached (Facebook), so it is an easy metric to find. Be wary of falling into the trap of reviewing all the additional engagement metrics at this time. For optimization of your social presence, these metrics can matter, although reactions (Like, Love, HaHa, Angry) have often been dubbed vanity metrics.

Paid impressions are purchased ads, promoted social posts, and pay per click (PPC) search terms for search engines: Bing,

Google, Yahoo, Baidu. All these platforms will have analytics in which the number of impressions served can be found.

Radio

Radio impressions can be the most difficult to measure. In Canada, there are two ways to receive objective information: Nielsen and Numeris. Your local radio rep may provide you with the reach-based population in the area coverage, but that is typically an unsubstantiated number.

Numeris employs Portable People Meters using statistically sound population samples to generate user listening habits and statics. The information is available online free for all to view. The challenge is that the metrics that are captured are not a unique impression number that print, online, or television can provide. The audience metrics available are: Average Minute Audience (AMA) and Daily Cum (the number of unique audience members daily) Share (the percentage of total hours tuned that a station receives of the total market listening hours). To calculate the number of unique listeners that would have heard the 30-second spot that you placed three times daily for 30 days is not possible, but total impressions is. If you had 90 spots, you simply calculate the total impressions as 90 × AMA. With this number, you will have to settle on total impressions as the only true metric, as opposed to unique impressions that can be reasonably calculated with other platforms.

Video

Digital video impressions are easy to tabulate. Regardless of the platform, there will be metrics on the number of views, whether via Facebook, YouTube, your own website, or digital pre-roll media buys, as you will pay per impression.

Traditional video (television) has been obsessively tracking viewership for decades, as with radio, Numeris is the primary provider of data. The statistics are quite detailed and the media buys report CPM (cost per thousand impressions), allowing you to easily tabulate your reach.

Direct Marketing

Direct marketing is a form of advertising in which organizations provide physical marketing materials to consumers to communicate information about a product or service. Direct marketing formats include flyers or catalogues or offer cards delivered directly to a consumer. The number of impressions is easy to calculate as a significant part of the promotion cost is the delivery. The cost of delivery is a derivative of the number of consumers delivered to. Thus, determining impressions is straightforward.

Out-of-Home

Out-of-Home (OOH) Advertising is any medium that is display advertising "outside of a consumer's home" such as billboards, posters, wallscapes, bus and rail media, street furniture, specialty signage, digital, mobile billboards, or aircraft. The versatility of out of home is that it can be anywhere, shown to anyone, at any time. The types of out of home advertising fall into four main media formats: billboards, street furniture, transit, or place based. For more details, browse the Outdoor Advertising Association of America's website, which is excellent and makes a compelling case for OOH use.

The challenge for marketers using OOH has long been measurement. The industry provides statistically sound measures regarding traffic passing within view of a format, but at the end of the day, it is uncertain as to whether the ad was seen. For impressions, you must be willing to accept estimates for these formats, based on data provided by the industry.

Events

Trade shows, closed private meetings, in-person customer training seminars; this channel includes any event to which people physically show up. The number of unique impressions is simply the attendance of the event, although in the case of a trade shows or consumer shows, consideration must be given to the fact that the entire gate attendance is not going to "see" your booth. So a reasonable estimate will be required.

KPI #2: CONVERSION

The rate represented as a percentage or decimal in which the outcomes of one activity "converts" to an action for the next step.

In this context, conversion is the percentage of impressions that "convert" into a lead. To track the conversion rate of a given channel, you need to know how to measure attribution for each channel by lead. In today's crowded messaging marketplace, tracking leads has become more complex. The easiest way to track leads is to determine how to create attribution, and use the last touch method. "Last touch" means that when a lead is received, the last channel touch that brought the lead to the brand counts for attribution. This is a simple method however, it does not tell the whole story in today's multimedia environment. By using last touch attribution, fairly or unfairly, some of your promotion efforts may not receive the attribution they deserve.

Imagine that your recreational customer Rick is looking for a motorcycle. Rick is driving home from work one day and hears an ad for a motorcycle on the radio. The ad creates an impression and reminds Rick he has always wanted a bike. After hearing the ad, Rick notices a billboard for the bike show next weekend. That night, he goes online and finds out more details of the bike show. During the week, Rick sees an ad while he is scrolling through the news feed on one of his social aps. He clicks on it and goes to the company landing page and learns more, but does not reach out to the company. He figures he will see them at the tradeshow over the weekend.

Rick goes to the show, talks to a salesperson, and sits on the bike he wants, but does not buy. He needs to talk things over with his wife first. Another week goes by. Rick and his wife have talked, and he has decided to buy a bike. Rick returns to the website of the company and sends in a request to be contacted. A second salesperson contacts him. When the salesperson asks how Rick found out about the company, Rick replies, "I went to your website", which the salesperson, Jerry, selects from a drop-down in the CRM menu.

As this was a lead from the website, the data lines up, but is this last touch attribution model fair and accurate?

Should the other channels in this example be given more credit? What about the radio ad that triggered the string of events, or the online offer? Or the 30 minutes of direct communication with a physical demonstration of the product at the tradeshow? As a result of these valid concerns, some marketers acknowledge that attribution for a lead is not simply the result of one touch on one channel, and therefore apply a weighted distribution of attribution. For example, the last touch receives 50% of the attribution and the remaining channels receive an equal fraction of the remaining 50%. Without software to automate this attribution, however, the calculations can become manually onerous. The choice to allocate attribution ultimately depends on your buyer journey and what will be the most accurate representation.

The methods of tracking attribution always revolve around the action of conversion. Is the customer calling, sending in a web form, texting, or coming in person to a physical location? Below are the main methods of tracking leads and creating attribution.

Call tracking

The are many services that can provide a brand with unique phone numbers that can be tracked and reported upon. The simplest use case is a print ad with a custom call tracking number. By simply counting the number of calls at the end of a tracking period (generally a month) you will have a feel for whether the ad is working. Call tracking does not have to be limited to print; all your mediums can have unique numbers, and therefore you can understand where your call volume comes from: your website, your Google My Business page, social media, your vehicle decaling, the list is as long as the list for segmentation for call attribution and is only limited by your resources and imagination.

Discount or coupon codes

Another classic example of creating attribution: if you run an offer, no matter the channel, with a unique discount or coupon code for that channel, then you know the channel works or does not work based on redemptions of the discount or coupon code. Often this is done by campaign, integrating the marketing offer (discount or coupon code) across multiple channels, so that lessens the direct attribution—though the theory holds. Create a unique offer and then tally the results whether on per channel or per campaign basis.

Microsites/landing pages/vanity URLs

These three destinations are an alternate way to channel consumer actions online so more effective attribution and conversion can occur (in the case of microsites and landing pages).

A vanity URL is merely a redirect URL to your main website. The URL is often specifically named to be memorable for the customer and the offer such as companynovmaddness.com (hence the term vanity) An example of this use is placing a vanity URL in a print ad so that when a consumer acts on the ad they go to the vanity URL and that action and later actions due to UTM codes can be tracked for attribution for that ad. Without the use of vanity URLs, or a microsite or landing pages, traditional advertising will drive consumers to a company website and the marketing team will not know why they came to the site. The only attribution a marketer can track without these techniques is to see an increase in web traffic for a given period.

Microsites/landing pages are best practices used by marketers for conversion. Landing pages are custom pages made with basic information and a clear call to action, and are designed to get the customer to convert (call, email, download, etc.). They are often tested to determine which variation converts at a higher rate. Microsites are much the same, and offer in-depth information about a product or service that the main website or landing page does not allow for. For attribution, landing pages and microsites solve the issue of understanding where online traffic came from. Landing pages, in particular, can be created on a per-ad basis. Best-use scenarios are to use landing pages for PPC advertising or other display advertising. The attributions in these cases are basically a straight line, and thus are easily tallied if your online analytics are set up in accordance with the methods you are using.

UTM codes (Urchin Tracking Module)

A UTM code is a simple code that you can attach to a custom URL in order to track a source, medium, terms (paid search), and campaign name. It is this code that enables Google Analytics to tell you where searchers came from, as well as what campaign directed them to your website, microsite, or landing page. Google Analytics provides a tool to build custom campaign URLs with these UTM codes.

As stated previously, a common use of UTM codes is to create a vanity URL for each offline campaign, and then redirect that URL to whatever forwarding address you assign to it—most likely your main domain. This will give you the ability to track how a weekly newspaper ad, coupon, radio ad, or TV commercial is working, without having to create custom landing pages for each campaign. UTM codes used with call tracking will allow for your main URL to refresh to display unique phone numbers depending on the advertising source. This again allows for another layer of attribution.

Submission forms

Forms off your various online properties are an easy method for tracking. The old practice of having a generic email online for customer contact does not allow for the email source to be tracked. Submission forms can be tagged by UTM codes or made available only on specific landing pages, thus allowing for attribution.

SMS (Short Messaging System) short codes with opt in

Mobile marketing has increased in popularity as the use of mobile phones has propagated, to the point that they have now become universal. Statistics from Innovista Law's April 2018 *TCPA Survival Guide* easily highlight why this is becoming a trend:

- **99% of text messages are opened.**

- **90% are read within 3 minutes.**

- **40% get a response within 15 minutes.**

Compare those numbers with **email's 20% open rate**—and much lower response rates—and you can see why text message advertising is an important marketing method that businesses are increasingly turning to. The method for tracking by channel includes the use of short codes, opt ins, and landing pages within the offers.

The key is that this channel can be used as acquisition tracking for other channels, such as radio and out of home, and then further as a channel in of itself once opt in is provided by the customer. A typical attribution method would be an opt in with a short code over a radio ad. "To receive this month's special discount text 'Car' to 667788." One of the advantages of short codes is that vanity short codes can be purchased to make them more memorable; for instance, the message could be changed to be "text 'cheese' to Mario's [the restaurant name] to receive your discount code."

CRM data

When the customer finally directly contacts the brand and begins the sale process, as part of the process your customer-facing staff should ask: "And what brought you in today?" If a list of channels is provided, the rep can quickly select the channel indicated by the customer, and this data can be reported in correlation to leads, opportunities, and closed or lost deals. CRM data can close the loop for hard-to-track channels; however, there is the danger of inaccurate information being tracked and sales staff skewing results based on the questions they ask. For instance, sales staff can inadvertently lead a customer by asking "Did you hear our radio ad?" when trying to prompt the customer to explain what brought them in. The challenge is to be mindful and train your team so that data is not influenced, and remains objective.

With the total amount of leads tracked and determined by channel, only then can a conversion rate be determined. Recall that the conversion rate is the percentage of impressions that convert into a lead. With a known conversion rate, you can begin to tweak marketing to increase leads. If you increase your conversion rate and increase your leads, in theory you should increase your sales and number of customers.

The next question to answer is the rhythm of reporting for conversion. The answer is, of course, it depends. It depends on the length and intensity of a campaign. There have been times when I have tracked KPIs daily, but most commonly I review specific campaigns weekly and overall metrics monthly. The rhythm you choose will depend on the cycles of your business.

KPI #3: LEADS

The number of qualified potential customers that have taken an action are "converted," which indicates they have displayed a commercial intent with your organization.

You know how to track and tabulate leads on a per channel basis, and you have decided upon the reporting cycle by channel. The next step is to determine if all the lead opportunities are being captured. Consider this scenario: Your team calculates the leads for the previous week at 25 and you cross reference the new leads in your CRM at 15 leads. That is a 40% discrepancy! Where did the leads go?

This is a classic example of the gap between marketing and sales departments. One department will blame the other: either the leads were no good or the sales team did not capture the opportunity. In my experience, having been on both sides, the truth is usually in the middle. This gap represents an opportunity to increase the number of qualified captured leads without increasing marketing spend. All that is needed is training and teamwork between the departments, once the gap has been identified.

If you are using call tracking, the calls can be recorded. This represents game tape that can be reviewed and used to train teams. Perhaps the leads are not getting to the right person, or the leads are not fully qualified—though these still need to be captured so they can be nurtured with ongoing marketing automation.

As a leader, you will have to roll up your sleeves and dig into the challenge to find a way to close the gap. Depending on the software platforms you have access to, predictive analytics and AI are starting to help with lead scoring, providing yet another layer of understanding.

For example, one of my teams was recently able to determine

for a reporting period that 90% of the leads were good, qualified leads by using lead scoring based on natural language processing of recorded calls. Further, we were able to determine facts about the 10% that were not leads, such as the intent of the customer contact (which was seeking service), and then understand how the service calls were handled by the sales team. By digging into the lead metric, some customer experience issues were brought to light and could be addressed.

Remember, the big win only happens with tracking. Now you know there is a gap, whereas before you did not, and therefore the opportunity to improve was unknown.

KPI #4: CLOSE RATE

The percentage of leads that become a sale.

Calculating the next metric, closed deals, is simple arithmetic. The segmentation of data sets with this metric will provide the most insight. To start, you will want to know the aggregate close rate of your organization for a baseline. After that is determined, digging into segments such as location, product division, or rep will provide insights that can be actionable. With training, it is easy to focus on any lagging area to increase the close percentage. Segments that have a higher than average close rate can also be observed for insights into what is being done to obtain these higher rates.

As with all metrics, recording the results is merely the first step.

KPI #5: REVENUE

Data within revenue metrics over a set time period.

These metrics include a "set of eight" data points to review for signals: new customers, existing customers, average transaction size for new and existing customers, gross margin for new and existing customers, and number of transactions for new and existing customers.

To calculate these metrics, your accounting system/accounting team will need to be leveraged to create standardized reports. These numbers are the top line of your profit and loss statement; understanding them in the context of your customer journey sheds new light on their impact.

The insights gained by reporting your revenue metrics into the set of eight can be profound, as described in Section Two.

As you are setting up reports for your revenue metrics, your customer data needs to be mined to gain further insights into your customer journey. As part of this step, you will gather existing customer data beyond the set of eight data points. You will need to dive deeper by asking and answering questions about your customer data such as:

- Who are your key accounts and what is their lifetime value?

- Is there a clear rule like Pareto's 80/20 rule, in which 20% of your customers represent 80% of your revenue?

- What is the age of your key accounts?

- What is the average revenue per account (ARPA)? Is it increasing, stagnant, or declining?

- How many customers do you have?

As you answer the above questions, you will see patterns. All organizations are able to group their customers by buying patterns, demographics or use case. These groups can be used to create target market profiles (see Step 4). Simply put, a target market profile humanizes the data segmentation of your customers. For instance, in reviewing your customer data, you can create a list of customers that spend greater than X in a year, or a list of customers that buy multiple products and services, or a list of customers that only buy one type of product and service. Each of these lists may represent a target market profile.

The more information you can dig up about your customers, the more it will help you in understanding your organization's customer journey. Beyond your customer data, you will also need to know specific information for your industry. Much of this information is critical to providing context for the data about your customer journey. So be prepared to review some data and perform some calculations.

KPI #6: REPUTATION MANAGEMENT

The average rating your business receives on online review platforms, as provided by customers.

Reputation Management data is easy to gather, as it merely

needs to be set up and monitored. The challenge for many organizations is in obtaining a credible number of reviews. That number is often defined by industry and competition, but a minimum of double digits is typically deemed necessary.

As discussed in Section Two, the standard review platforms need to be managed, along with industry specific platforms. Most of these platforms can be set up to send alerts when reviews occur so you can respond to all reviews (good, simply acknowledge, bad, conduct service recovery, as outlined previously).

Starting the tracking of review platforms can be a manual process, and scores can be recorded in a spreadsheet. If your organization is a single location this may be all you need to do to start. However, if you are a multi-location organization, this type of manual management can quickly become overwhelming to the point that software becomes a must; happily, for organizations this emerging space has plenty of vendors to choose from.

Forrest Research defines customer feedback management software as:

> "A system of software and processes that supports a company's VoC program by helping a company to solicit feedback from key customers across channels; centrally collect solicited and unsolicited feedback; analyze structured and unstructured feedback; distribute insights across the organization; close the loop with customers; act on the insights; and monitor progress continuously."

The voice of the customer (VOC) is a term used in business and Information Technology to describe the process of capturing customer's expectations, preferences, and aversions.

These systems are inclusive for reputation management and social listening, and like the NPS will collect various customer satisfaction scores (C-SAT). They also help get reviews.

The first way to get reviews is to ask your customers to post a review, however, reviews will happen without encouragement if your experience falls on extremes (really good or really bad). As an organization, you do not want to rely on unprompted reviews. At the end of the day, in order to solicit reviews from your customers, you need basic contact data for your customers. To increase the likelihood of honest reviews and to receive timely feedback, the request for reviews should happen immediately after the transaction point in the customer journey. Think of your journey: when is the transfer point from buying to using? That is when you ask for a review. To secure online reviews, the methods fall into two camps: email solicitation and SMS solicitation. As previously stated, SMS has higher response rates, although it is a much more expensive channel. The key to receiving reviews is to ask. The method is up to you, and results you receive will be a direct derivative of your effort and your organization's emphasis.

KPI #7: NPS NET PROMOTER SCORE

A customer satisfaction metric that predicts referrals and repeat business.

There are many methods that can be used to gather NPS scores, and they depend on the nature of your business. Collecting the response is just part of a five-step C-SAT process:

1. Announce

2. Launch

3. Experience recoveries

4. Thank your customers

5. Watch for trends

Prior to launching an NPS program, you need to announce the program launch internally and externally. Internally, your staff must be trained to include program details in the sale process. Externally, you can create store signage and details on your web page indicating that customers will be surveyed. This announcement will aid in a higher acceptance and response rate. If a customer expects a survey with the intent of requesting their feedback to improve upon your service, the customer will be more likely to participate.

The main methods are calls (either outbound or diverted inbound calls) and digital, website based, or surveys (email or SMS). Collecting NPS scores by telephone falls under outbound after the sale and inbound diverted after the sales call.

Outbound calls use call center agents or a designated internal individuals or teams to collect data and perform the survey. The advantage of this process is if the agents/teams are trained and empowered in your customer recovery system, they can immediately begin to solve issues. Alternately, in some organizations the sales team is tasked with the NPS gathering. This is common in the auto industry, and the challenge is the bias of the data collected. Sales people tend to influence the NPS rating through "coaching" the customer, which in my opinion reduces the integrity of the survey.

Inbound diverted calls are dependent on the nature of your business. If conducting an NPS process makes sense at the end of a transactional call, the call can be diverted to an agent (or designated internal team member). Alternately, the customer can be diverted to an IVR (interactive voice response) survey system that will conduct the survey. While the score can be easily captured, the comments should be recorded and reviewed.

Digitally collected surveys can occur via email or SMS for outbound collection, or be app or web based for inbound collection.

For digital outbound collection, you will need a survey platform to send out an email or SMS with a link to a survey. SurveyMonkey is the ubiquitous survey platform that has an NPS module that can be purchased as a tool. Other tools focus specifically on NPS, such as Retently, and allow more customization. Some CRM/marketing automation platforms also have NPS functionality built in, so the process can be automated to be sent at the timeliest stage of the customer journey to receive the highest response rate. (For instance, a campaign can be set up to send an NPS three days after product delivery.) For SMS, as with email, you will need a platform (or you can custom build one) to manage the delivery and response to SMS messaging. Many existing platforms provide interaction with your customers to help with reputation management and VoC surveys. Text messaging can be timed for an optimal response rate within the customer journey. For example, an SMS message can be sent immediately after delivery of a product. The timing, combined with the customer expecting this to happen, should provide extremely high response rates.

Inbound digital collection methods include web or in-app pop ups, or tabs within a webpage or app, to prompt your customers to provide their voice about their experience by filling out an NPS questionnaire. These inbound pop-up collection methods can be viewed by customers as intrusive to their experience, however, so be cautious in their use.

In all cases, either sending or conducting surveys or diverting traffic to conduct surveys, as a brand you need to be prepared to act when you receive negative or poor responses. If you have resources available, you can begin to address negative customer experiences almost as they happen.

In addition, after the surveys have been sent and collected, you should thank your customers for responding with an independent process beyond the automated message at the end of the survey. This can be accomplished by using a loyalty gesture such as a discount code that they can use for future purchases.

Lastly, the NPS will need to be monitored for correlated trends. For instance, does the NPS lower when business volume picks up, or are there spikes downward with new hires? Both of these trends point to challenges within your team. As a rule, your NPS will directly correlate to your employee engagement. An interesting exercise to learn about your employee engagement is to conduct an ENPS (Employee NPS). If your Employee NPS is low, how do you think that shows up in the customer experience being provided?

It takes being curious with non-obvious insights to spot correlated trends, simply monitoring the direction of the NPS up or down is not enough, you need to delve into why.

KPI #8: CUSTOMER CHURN

The proportion of customers who leave your business during a given time period; the time period is often one year, although monthly and quarterly time periods are also common, depending on the industry.

Customer churn measures the number of customers that leave an organization either by not conducting repeat purchases or by cancelling subscription services. This metric is represented as a percentage. We are currently experiencing 40% customer churn, which means 40% of the customers that purchased or were subscribers in time period t did not purchase again in the following time period, or cancelled a subscription. The inverse of customer churn is retention rate. If there is a 40% churn, there is a 60% retention rate. Using the percentage as a ratio will tell you how many time periods equals your average customer lifespan. Considering the 40% churn was for an annual time period represented as t = 100, to calculate the average life span you simply need to divide period t (which will always = 100) by the churn rate. For example, the Average Lifespan = 100/40 = 2.5 time periods; in this example, the average customer lifespan is 2.5 years.

The collection of data to calculate this metric falls on your accounting system or CRM. In one of the two systems, you will need to tabulate the total customers in a set time period and then measure how many of those customers purchased in the subsequent time period. If you do not have built-in churn reporting or the ability to create a custom report, minor manual data manipulation will be required. One method is to export your data from several time periods into a spreadsheet, and then use simple sort and match functions to obtain the total number of retained customers.

When creating customer churn reports, in essence, you will be creating a customer churn model based on the reporting criteria you set up. Time period is one criterion, but you may wish to impose a minimum purchase size for a customer to be considered retained. The factors for the model you create will depend on your business and customer segments. Consider, for instance, factors for contractual (subscription) customers, which have a very visible churn event when they cancel their service versus the factors in your churn model for non-contractual customers who have a non-visible churn event; they simply stop purchasing from your brand. One size doesn't fit all; a little trial and error will be needed before your working model provides the insights that you need.

Step 2
SUMMARY AND REFLECTIONS

SUMMARY

While this book focuses on eight key metrics, gathering and collecting metrics creates insights and the need for further metrics.

This section reviewed how to set up and gather data "manually" if you currently do not have an integrated tech stack with marketing automation, a CRM, and an ERP. However, if you have a fully integrated tech stack and your data is clean, gathering these data points and more is simply a matter of setting up business intelligence dashboards. Beyond a "basic" integrated tech stack of marketing automation, CRM, and ERP, customer management platforms can map your customer journeys by creating customer profiles and producing metrics such as NPS and customer churn by profile and location. This information can easily be accessed by running a report or reviewing a system dashboard. Generally, this is the realm of larger enterprises. The scope of this book

is to provide an understanding of where and how to start, crawl, and walk before you run.

In the beginning, the first insights will revolve around what you have and do not have. There may be process changes required before you begin to gather the basic customer data you need to calculate these metrics. Happily, if you have not been measuring customer data in this fashion at all, any insights are going to create a groundswell of desire with upper management to gain more. Thus, it has been my experience that when you start to gather data, continuing is a downhill rather than an uphill push.

REFLECTIONS

- Document the data that you have and do not have.

- Of the data that you have, what metrics can be calculated?

- Of the data that you need, what will be the easiest to obtain? Start with the low-hanging fruit.

- Are there some data sets that are incomplete but still statistically relevant? If so, you can extrapolate. For instance, polling 20% of customers to provide an NPS is better than waiting for 100% of the data.

Step 3
SET GOALS AND MEASURE AGAINST THEM

YOU HAVE NOW defined one or several customer journeys for your organization, and have subsequently gathered data on the key metrics, to establish a baseline for your business. It is now time to set goals to measure against, and to learn what to do next.

To begin setting goals, you can use industry benchmarks as a standard to measure against. Using your current state as baseline, ask the question: *Is your organization higher than the industry standard or lower?* Simply knowing where you are and then where you are in comparison to your peers provides considerable insight about your performance. Furthermore, doing the comparison signals a culture shift, showing that you are willing to have your performance objectively measured. Without objective comparison, it is easy to fall into the "good enough" trap, because you are measuring and setting goals in your own vacuum. As stated by Jim Collins in his book *Good to Great*, "good is the enemy of great."

A willingness to be measured is the first key to creating

ongoing improvements. The classic management axiom, "if it gets measured, it gets managed," rings so true. By taking this step of measuring your entire customer journey, you are managing parts of your business that were never measured before. They just happened, and business continued on. Now, you know from the numbers how well points of your customer journey are performing, and you can now set goals to increase that performance.

Why set goals? Just like a plan, a goal gives you something to deviate against. If the goal is hit or missed, you now have a result you can learn from. The goal becomes your internal benchmark to measure against as you reflect upon results. The goals you set do not always have to be about improvement. For instance, you can have goals to never let your NPS fall below 40 (industry average for retail according to SurveyMonkey benchmarks) or your missed call-backs to never exceed 5%. It all depends on the needs of your business and its maturity level with customer experience management.

BEST PRACTICE

BENCHMARKING

There is great value in benchmarking, and great folly at the same time. Finding the data on an industry leader, or at the very least a lateral comparable industry, is pretty easy. Many software tools you will use to gather information on your customer or to interact with your customers will have benchmarks built in. SurveyMonkey or MailChimp, for instance, both have comparative statistics on industries at your fingertips. Alternately, if you join industry associations, specific metrics for the industry are often available. Professional associations can also provide data to benchmark against. If you need sales data, reach out to a professional sales organization like the CPSA (Canadian Professional Sales Association), or for CX data try the CXPA (Customer Experience Professionals Association). Major consultancies such as McKinsey and Company, and Forrester's also have reams of data that is often freely published that can be searched.

Benchmarking against an industry leader as a goal setting exercise, however, can be pure folly. Indeed, this idea doesn't make sense to me. If I were to take an industry leader and use their NPS from yesterday as a goal, to reach it might take me several years. The problem with this type of action is that I would most likely be behind that leader by the same amount in the future as I was when I pegged my organization against that leader initially. The benchmarking, therefore, did not improve my organization in comparison to my peers. My organization would have merely treaded water.

Benchmarking, however, does give you context from which to set your own goals. What I do like about the SurveyMonkey and MailChimp benchmarks is that they are constantly updating. Thus, as the industry improves in real time from use of their platforms, their benchmarks adjust. In this context, these benchmarks help provide a reality check as to the actions you are taking.

Now that you have been mining and gathering data on your customer journey, you can place the current state into a goal worksheet. With your current data populated and your research into industry benchmarks completed as a point of reference, the fun begins. Goal setting is deciding the future of your organization.

With current data, you can set goals on a per metric basis for improvement, but it should be acknowledged that for all for profit enterprises, cash is king, and cash originates from revenue. This framework allows you to set goals working backwards from customers or revenue numbers as all the first two stages metrics are derivative of each other.

Consider the following goal for time period t:

Revenue Goal	$100,000
Historical average transaction size:	$1,500

With the goal of $100,000 and an ATS of $1,500, by working backwards, 67 sales are required to hit this goal.

Now you can create goals based on reach, conversion, leads, and close rate to secure the $100,000 in revenue.

If the close rate is 20%, 67/0.2 = 334 leads are required.

If the conversion rate is 3%; 334/0.03 = 11,111 reach impressions are required.

Working backwards within this framework, you now know what you need to do to achieve your goal of $100,000 in revenue. Populate your goal worksheet and measure the outcomes to start learning how to improve.

GOAL WORKSHEET   STEVE WHITTINGTON

MARKET SEGMENT _____

COMPANY OPERATION _____

METRICS	CURRENT	PERIOD 1 GOALS	ACTUALS	VARIANCE	VARIANCE %
REACH					
CONVERSION RATE					
LEADS					
CLOSE RATE					
REVENUE					
AVERAGE TRANSACTION					
CUSTOMERS					
REPUTATION RATING					
NPS					
CHURN					

Download this graphic and more at stevewhittington.com

EXAMPLE GOAL WORKSHEET

STEVE WHITTINGTON

MARKET SEGMENT RECREATIONAL ATV

COMPANY OPERATION POWERSPORTS DIVISION

METRICS	CURRENT	PERIOD 1 GOALS	ACTUALS	VARIANCE	VARIANCE %
REACH	5,000,000	5,500,000	4,700,000	-800,000	-14.55%
CONVERSION RATE	1.30%	1.60%	1.65%	0.05%	3.13%
LEADS	65000	88000	77550	-10,450	-11.88%
CLOSE RATE	15%	15%	18%	3%	20.00%
REVENUE	$12,187,500.00	$16,500,000.00	$17,448,750.00	$948,750.00	5.75%
AVERAGE TRANSACTION	1250	1250	1250	0	0.00%
CUSTOMERS	9750	13200	13959	759	5.75%
REPUTATION RATING	3.5	4	4	0	0.00%
NPS	41	45	50	5	11.11%
CHURN	70%	65%	61%	-4%	-6.15%

Download this graphic and more at stevewhittington.com

When setting goals, you will have to determine reporting periods. I recommend periods of no more than a quarter. The pace of reporting will be the pace of improvement. If you report quarterly, your pace of improvement will be every quarter. If you report every month, your pace of improvement will be monthly. There are cases for certain customer initiatives that I have been part of that use daily reporting, and weekly has also been common.

Whatever time period you choose, you will begin to illuminate touchpoints that require improvement. Cross-referencing the variance results of this worksheet with the Customer Journey map worksheet will highlight touchpoints and processes that require improvement. Within several reporting cycles, this will become clear, and your organization will now have knowledge for the next steps in the transformation process.

Lastly, make all your goals SMART—Specific, Measurable, Attainable, Realistic, Timely. By definition, this framework covers the SMT. With regards to the "AR", go gentle at the beginning when you are learning about your customer journey. If you are well below industry average, is it realistic to set goals that will reach industry average in a short time period? Setting unrealistic goals can be self-defeating to your team, so it is important to be mindful during this process.

Step 3
SUMMARY AND REFLECTIONS

SUMMARY

GOALS DRIVE PERFORMANCE. They provide direction and understanding of how to reach results. The customer journey framework provides a working model for you to understand which weak links are thwarting your performance. Once you shine a light on these areas through goal setting, reviews, and performance measurements, you are armed with knowledge to start the work of corrective action.

REFLECTIONS

- Who are you going to set goals with? What does that process look like in your organization?

- Consider that if you set goals alone, they are your goals; if you set goals with your team, they are the team's goals.

- What are the cycles of your business? What reporting time periods are needed in order to sync your business and current reporting processes? How much workload will the reporting require (this depends on the systems your organization has in place)?

Step 4
CREATE TARGET MARKET PROFILES

THE FIRST FOUR steps focus on understanding your current state (as is). With the first three steps complete, you have mapped your customer journeys, or at least one, set up data to measure your customer journey, and have now begun to set goals to enhance your customer journey. The very process of setting improvement goals will enhance your journey.

You are now ready for Step 4: Create Target Market Profiles. Many Customer Experience professionals believe this step needs to come first, before any customer journey mapping is done. I agree, with the caveat that creating target market profiles needs to be done before you design your future (to be) customer journeys, but not before you map your current state (as is) journeys, as I believe you will need the touch-points of a current journey to help you best understand your customer.

To design your future state (to be) customer journeys, you need to base the design on facts and research into your organization and customers as opposed to hypotheses, assumptions, and hopes, which is all an organization has until it does the work of mapping the current state, gathering data, and segmenting revenue to understand current customers. Only after all of this work, is an organization ready to create target market profiles backed by research and data.

Creating target market profiles opens another set of possibilities for an organization. What more could you do as an organization if you knew more about your various customer segments? Could you personalize your messaging? Offer complementary products? Streamline their services?

To start to create target market profiles you need to list all the target markets and market segments that your organization is in. At this point, I must note that most of the theory on target market profiles—or buyer personas as they are alternatively called—has been conducted for acquisition marketing tactics.

Thus, in that mindset, marketing is identifying the segment within a target market that your organization wishes to reach.

Let's use the example of an educational book publishing house as the brand. Their target market could be education faculty; further dialed in, the market segment within this target market might be post-secondary education faculty focused on early child learning in Canada. This narrower focused description is often called the ideal customer profile. Simply put who or what type of organization would you ideally like to sell to, or that you feel is ideally suited for your products or services.

Further to the ideal customer profile, the specific individual that would be making the buying decision within that post-secondary education faculty needs to be described in detail. This level of detail is the Target Market Profile (or alternately, the buyer persona). The hierarchical waterfall goes as follows:

Target Market →

Market Segment (or Ideal Customer Profile) →

Target Market Profile

Begin by listing the target markets your organization does business in and the market segments within each of those target markets. Once the market segments are identified, document what your ideal customer in these segments actually represents. This ideal customer is a real customer. You have that customer, you just have to find them in your data. Give that "ideal customer" a name, a job, some demographics; humanize this customer in this market segment, and you are on your way to creating a target market profile.

WHAT IS A TARGET MARKET PROFILE?

A Target Market Profile is a complete sketch of a key segment of your customers/audience that provides deep understanding of that customer and allows an organization to interact with that segment in a meaningful manner that will create connection and loyalty.

The profile includes the basic demographics of age and gender, but goes deeper with name, job, attributes such as marital status, vehicle, recreation. The profile also dives into that individuals' attitudes (extroverted or introverted) and professional attitudes (work to live, or live to work) and their motivational drivers.

Keep in mind that you are creating an *individual* that represents a *segment* of your customers. The more you understand about your customer, the better you will be able to design a journey for them. For instance, if one of their motivators is quality you may wish to put more attention to a final selling inspection and client training to increase the perceived quality of the experience.

Creating target market profiles can get very in depth. The Canadian Marketing Association teaches combining personality archetypes (broadly defined as universal human ways of being) with ideal customer profiles to create a Target Marketing Profile. The sample target market profile included in this book is based off CMA best practices. For more information on archetypes go to:

https://www.sparkol.com/en/Blog/The-12-brand-archetypes-all-successful-businesses-are-built-on

At the end of this process, you should have three to five target market profiles and an understanding of services and products that each profile purchases from you, the percentage of sales this profile represents, and key messages that resonate with that profile. This deep understanding of your customers will help you improve your customer journey.

BEST PRACTICE

EXCERPT: SAMPLE TARGET MARKET PROFILE

Recreational Athlete: Target Market Profile

The Warrior

Name: Ryan

Gender: Male

Age: 25

Job: Journeyman electrician

Attributes: Single, drives a Honda Civic, loves playing and watching sports, athletic and fitness minded
Attitudes: Extroverted, proud, hardworking, determined, focused, goal/achievement oriented

The recreational athlete is a young adult who plays sports in his free time and on weekends. He played sports as a child and teen, and while he did not make a career of it, he continues to enjoy the athletic achievements and comradery that come from team sports. He works hard to maintain his skills and athleticism by working out in his free time. He enjoys the challenges and goal setting that come from playing sports and working out—he wants to achieve his personal best. He plays in a "beer league" but takes his games seriously. He will probably be the team captain of his rec team and enjoys encouraging others to play their best. He is competitive (and often with himself), but understands at the end of the day that this is a recreation league.

Motivational Drivers:

- Wants equipment that will meet and enhance his fitness goals (building muscle and endurance goals). Wants specific equipment for his home that he may not always find at a gym.

- Budget conscious: Equipment that offers multiple workouts or uses will be preferred.

- He is interested in keeping his body fit and in good shape, for athletic reasons but also to remain physically attractive.

Online Habits: Will shop online for research, but will come in to store to see the product quality. Good candidate for remarketing. Will ask friends/teammates on social media for recommendations. Will look to see what equipment the pro athletes are using. Social accounts: Instagram, Twitter, Snapchat.

Key Messaging Words: Results, goals, save money, save time, achieve, best, athletic, versatile, multi-use

Words to Own: Strength training, CrossFit, cross

training, home gym, dumbbells, weights, weight lifting, weight bench, power cage, plyobox, cardio machines, Bowflex, SelectTech, treadmill

Projection: 15% of Customer Sales

Depending on the size and scope of the organization, there may be many profiles that need to be written, or just three to five. If there are five or fewer, roll up your sleeves and do the work. When creating profiles, gather a cross-functional group that touches the customer through your customer journey. Have the data on your current state journeys available, and be open to brainstorm the attributes of your customers.

If you have more than five customer profiles, you will need to prioritize. The two factors to start with are volume of transactions a profile represents and total revenue volume a profile represents. These two factors often correlate, but can be mutually exclusive, depending on the business. The other factor to consider pertains to which profile represents the highest growth; again, this factor can correlate with the previous two, or be mutually exclusive. The last factor to consider looks at customers that are taken for granted (every organization has a customer profile like this). This customer profile generally does not represent a lot of effort for the organization to deal with, and is often considered the "easy customer." The easy customer often represents an organization's base; that customer base of an organization should never be forgotten or ignored.

Considering these four factors, as a starting point, there may be four customer groups to create profiles for:

1. High Volume Transaction Customers

2. High Revenue Customers

3. High Growth Customers

4. Easy Customers

If any organization obsessively focuses on improving the customer experience for these four groups, their results will improve. After creating the target market profiles for the organization's customer segments, designing the future (to be) customer journeys can begin.

Step 4
SUMMARY AND REFLECTIONS

SUMMARY

WITH THE FIRST four steps complete, you are now ready to begin designing your future (to be) customer journeys. You have selected market segments to profile that represent the largest portion of your customers either by volume, revenue, opportunity, or those that represent your base. You have created target market profiles for these segments to gain a deeper understanding of them. Armed with the current state of your organization, data, goals and their outcomes, you can use target market profiles to design a future state journey that will transform your business.

REFLECTIONS

- How many market segments do you have? One way to start to tally this is to add up the different products and services you sell that are, or can be, mutually exclusive.

- What is the biggest portion of your customers by volume? By revenue?

- What were your first customers like? Do they still buy from you today? If so, that is your loyal customer base.

Step 5
DESIGN YOUR CUSTOMER JOURNEY

AT THIS POINT, you have your current state mapped, data gathered, target market profiles created, and goals set to measure results against. You now know where the pain points are, and you are excited to fix them.

The next step is to pick a journey and gather the cross-functional team that currently executes the touchpoints of that journey. With the team in place and the pain points determined, now is the time to brainstorm to reduce customer and employee effort. Time to make things better! Right?

Wrong. The vagueness of this last statement proves a point; what are you going to specifically improve upon? Before you map, you need to have an improvement goal to work towards. Digital marketing professionals use A/B testing for optimizing conversion rates of ads or landing pages. A/B testing is very precise and subtle. To ensure a clear understanding of what is causing the improvement or reduction in conversion rates, only one aspect of an ad or landing page is changed for testing. This could be font size, font color, one or two words in messaging, color of a button or placement of the call to action button. The point is only one change is made to note the incremental impact, and then, based on those results, the next incremental change is made, and so and so on.

I am not suggesting that you neglect obvious pain points that need to be addressed. The point is to be aware that small changes can make a disproportionate impact and thus nothing should be overlooked for improvement when designing your new journeys.

Some "small" areas to focus on in your processes for improvements include consistency, wait times, customer effort, greetings, and closures. Most of these areas are people-dependent and can seem minor to an overall journey. It is often stated, however, that business results occur because of two things: people and processes. Ultimately, the spirit in which your people execute the processes divides their degrees of excellence.

Let me explain. I am often fond of telling people when reviewing their customer experience that being friendly is free. Take a touchpoint of greeting a customer: An individual can say, "Hello, how can I help you?" with cheer or with annoyed brevity. The exact same words may have been spoken, so the process is executed as prescribed, but the intent and the impact are far different. Imagine if the next touchpoint in the journey sets the tone of bored indifference or uninterested impatience, even though qualifying questions are asked. If one were to listen to this recorded interaction, the outcome from the customer satisfaction score would be clearly apparent as opposed to the bafflement that the poor score is greeted with by staff that have executed the processes according to the letter of the training guide.

People and processes dictate the results of an organization. This is why when you map it is important to have data from the journey along the path, so these smallest details can be identified. Sometimes the customer journey does not need to be changed, merely more training should be provided to people executing the processes or more support and resources provided. If a step in the journey is taking an unreasonable amount of time, perhaps support is merely required to the staff executing the process, so that it can occur faster. Or if the particular step requires a fair amount of customer effort, try to eliminate it or find a way to support the customer so the effort required can be reduced. Generally, many process improvements are subject to technology. Your staff may need access to timely and detailed information to provide a better customer experience. In this case, the support your staff needs will be a management information system. While all business improvements are a derivative of people and processes, technology and data can be limiting constraints that are holding back your star, customer facing staff.

With these considerations in mind, and a current state customer journey displayed for all to see with the pain points highlighted, now is the time to grab a blank template and decide upon the goal you are trying to achieve. With the goal in mind, you can begin to design. Ideally, the goal aligns with corporate strategy, however, it is a rare feat that improving a customer experience does not align with corporate strategy.

Goals to consider may be increasing the number of customers served per day, decreasing the length of time for customer processes (such as web forms or wait lines). These goals, by default, must be tied back to increasing customer satisfaction—and more importantly to the eight KPIs.

There are only a few steps to follow when designing a new customer journey:

1. **Requirement gathering:** This includes the current state maps and data for this customer journey.

2. **Select a cross-functional team:** Individuals that represent the different touchpoints need to be included when designing the customer journey. They will provide insights, and including them will provide buy-in to the new processes to allow for their future execution, with optimal intent.

3. **Have a goal to rally the design around:** Keep in mind the goal is always tied to one of the eight KPIs so that outcomes can be objectively measured. For instance, if the goal is to reduce wait times there could be several KPIs to measure: reputation management, NPS, and customer churn. When looking at the current state and data, it may be obvious what the goal should be. If that is the case, wonderful! State the goal and design your new journey to achieve that goal. If the goal is not obvious there will always be pain points to fix. Fixing these pain points can be the goal in and of itself. Be sure to harvest the benefits of these fixed pain points by tying them to a KPI.

4. **Create a shared blank canvas:** Blank white walls and sticky notes are an amazing canvas for designing customer journeys. Find a space with your team and start filling it up.

5. **Ask stretch questions:** Ask questions like those of the founder of Airbnb: What would a 3 out 5 experience look like? What would a 4 out 5 experience look like? What would a 5 out of 5 experience look like? What would a 6 out of 5 experience look like? These questions can create "out of the box" thinking that opens up further possibilities.

6. **Design from outside in first:** Once you have created the ideal customer journey review the journey inside out to learn the processes, people and required technology to be implemented.

7. **Review this new journey with your customers**. Even though you and your team believe you have improved the customer experience with this new map, validate the new map with existing customers. Your customers, if asked, will point out pain points and what works and doesn't work for the "new" designed journey. Seeking customer understanding prior to implementation is a critical step that is all too often ignored. The old adage *"the customer is always right"* is very appropriate for this context.

8. **Have fun!** Laughter leads to people opening up and sharing ideas. Enjoy the process, because together, you and your team are making your customer's experience and your team's environment better.

Step 5
SUMMARY AND REFLECTIONS

SUMMARY

ORGANIZATIONS THRIVE WHEN three outcomes align: what is good for the customer, what is good for the employee, and what is good for the enterprise. Keep these three legs of the stool in mind when designing journeys. Journey mapping takes time, and creating a new journey is only the beginning. When creating designs, consideration for training, technology and implementation must occur.

REFLECTIONS

When picking the first journey to design, ask the following questions:

- Which customer journey in the organization has the greatest amount of "pain" for the customers?

- Which customer journey could be altered the fastest to show immediate positive results?

- Which customer journey does your staff believe is
  the most painful for them to execute upon?

The answers to these three questions will hopefully intersect
and provide clarity for where you need to start.

INSIGHT

SAMPLE CUSTOMER JOURNEY DESIGN

A simple example of designing a customer journey
touchpoint, using the three questions above, was for
an e-commerce website. The pick up in store delivery
option was creating a negative employee and customer
experience, due to the expectations of the customer
and the requirements of the staff to fulfill the customer expectations.

For this organization, the issue was all about communication (or lack thereof). A customer would order a
product for free in store pick up and expect the product to available the same day, or often within the hour.
Logistically, the organization was not able to fill this
expectation 100% of the time. As a result, on occasion
both customers and customer-facing staff were frustrated with the online process. Of course, as the number of instances cumulated, so too did the internal

frustration. A simple tweak to the process mitigated the ongoing situation.

The online process was changed from "Pick up in store" to "Ship to store" with supporting customer communication when the online order confirmation was sent. This changed the customer expectation and eliminated over 90% of the frustrated customer expectations.

When designing this change, the KPI goal was to increase the NPS. Within a few reporting periods the NPS did indeed increase.

One simple tweak in the customer journey eliminated customer pain, staff pain, and created immediate results when implemented.

Find intersection points in your customer journey and results far greater than the effort of the change will follow.

Step 6
IMPLEMENT

THE GREATEST CHALLENGE with any new process and cultural shift is the fact of its newness. The roll-out of your new customer experience program really is the first step to "baking in" customer-centric thinking across your organization. The classic change management tactics apply to a new customer experience initiative.

For your customer experience transformation to have the greatest chance of success, it is important to establish buy-in from the very top to at least 51% of your staff prior to starting to measure and designing new journeys. This is accomplished by justifying the change, and then acquiring the resources needed to execute, followed up by an intensive communication plan. Only when these steps are in place, can you begin to implement change initiatives. For customer experience initiatives, I recommend the following seven steps for implementation.

IMPLEMENTATION STEP 1: JUSTIFICATION: STATING THE WHY

Change is always resisted, so to overcome that resistance, a good reason for change must be communicated clearly. In the case of customer experience (CX), it may be declining profits; if that is the case, the drop in profits represents a pain point to rally around, from which to build a business case. To start, it goes without saying you need top-down buy-in. The first group that needs to be convinced is the executive team. A business case will need to be prepared for that audience. Generally, to convince executives, you will need some basic data showcasing the pitfalls of your current customer experience. At the very beginning, the change leader will need to dig deep and do the extra work to convince others to get more resources to carry on the work. Often, when implementing change, you will need to build your case unsupported until executive buy-in and resources are achieved.

The next group is your general staff. A business case about profitability does not land as well with front line staff; however, an initiative that will reduce customer effort and increase customer satisfaction while at the same time enhancing the employee experience will. Business is about people and processes. Your team will respond to an initiative that will give them the tools to make people (their customers) smile. I recommend this style of justification to be used when you roll out the initiative to the full staff.

IMPLEMENTATION STEP 2: ALLOCATION OF RESOURCES

Once the business case is approved, a dedicated team should be assembled with access to sufficient resources to make the change come to life. If you start an initiative without ample resources to make an impact, your customer experience transformation will just be another flavour of the month corporate initiative that bubbles up and then goes away. You will need leaders, teachers, front-line customer-facing staff and individuals collecting data, and the systems for data collection in place, to make your CX transformation happen. This cross-functional team will execute all the pre-steps of mapping the current state, mining your data, setting goals, measuring, and creating target market profiles. After the rollout to all staff, additional cross-functional teams can be created to design new journeys, measure the results and iterate.

IMPLEMENTATION STEP 3: COMMUNICATION TO ALL STAKEHOLDERS

Before the initiative kicks off, as part of your justification the more layers of management that are involved, the better. This creates a base of support for the initiative's launch. In other words, to start, your communication will involve plenty of one-to-one talks to build buy-in. Once that base is created, only then do you communicate one-to-many. This communication of a customer experience initiative should come from a senior leader, ideally the CEO or President. That shows top-level buy-in and support. A mistake for the one-to-many mass communication is to include the announcement in regular communication channels (quarterly newsletter, annual update, etc.). This new initiative should receive an independent message, such as a letter to all staff or even a video for all to watch. Pick the medium that works best for your audience.

IMPLEMENTATION STEP 4: ROLL OUT

When you start this initiative, everyone in the organization needs to be touched and trained. A series of town hall meetings with mandatory attendance and a schedule can get everyone informed and working in the same direction. This roll out can include justification and an introduction to customer experience and why it matters. By this point, you should have some real data that shows the good and bad of your current processes; clear real organization information always lands far more effectively than conceptual theories. Share the good, the bad, and the ugly, and then share the vision for the future you will pursue together.

IMPLEMENTATION STEP 5: CREATION OF NEW PROCESSES

This is where Step 5: Design Your Customer Journey, comes into play. By reviewing the data you have collected and the current journeys you have mapped, some obvious quick wins should be evident. Pick your top one to three journeys and design new journeys with cross-functional teams, as described in Step 5.

IMPLEMENTATION STEP 6: TRAINING AND SUPPORT

With new journeys created, a training and measurement plan can be built to implement these new journeys. If you have done all the previous steps well, your team will be primed and waiting for this change to occur. Typical training requirements for roll outs of new customer journeys go as follows.

First and most importantly, all team members involved in a customer touchpoint must be gathered and trained in the new process for this journey, in addition to the data collection and measurement methods that will be occurring. The team leader will observe the on-the-job implementation of the process for hands-on training support. The outcomes will be measured, and ongoing spot checks need to be implemented to ensure the new process is being followed. It generally takes 30 days for a new action to become a habit; be sure to allocate at least that time frame for training and support for each new journey implementation.

As importantly, do not overload individuals or service groups with more than one process change at a time. This way, they can focus and "see" the differences of the one new process compared with previous processes. They will be able to compare the positive outcomes of this new process to the processes that have yet to be changed. This comparison should get them excited and engaged for the next new journey to be unveiled.

IMPLEMENTATION STEP 7: ONGOING RESULTS AND CASE STUDIES

Creation of a shared space and rhythm of review is critical to any new process' chance of success. In the past, physical "war rooms" would be set up where all reports and documents were housed, in which the team could gather to review. With multi-location businesses this is not possible, and even with single location businesses, space may be a consideration. Creating a "war room" in the cloud that the entire team can access 24/7 meets this need. Whether you use Google Docs and folders or Office 365, OneDrive, and SharePoint sites, the purpose of the cloud functionality is the same. What is needed is a shared space in which documentation, measurement of results, and customer stories can be consolidated around the new journeys being implemented.

Timely, constant, consistent communication is critical for a new process to be established. For me, this means at minimum weekly meetings with the implementation team to review what is working and what is not working, addressing challenges, and reviewing ongoing results to glean insights that lead to committed action items with completion dates documented and agreed upon.

For some change initiatives, at the start I have used a daily huddle to kick start the "baking in" of the process. A daily huddle focused on the customer journey is a powerful way to share customer success stories and pain points that have popped up, and gives an opportunity to address them. Some of these pain points will not require a process change, just awareness. Thus, daily meetings can really ramp up the pace of improvement and reinforce a culture centered on the customer.

Setting up a dashboard to showcase results versus goals can be as simple as a graph of data from an Excel file or as complex as multiple data sources being integrated in reporting platforms like Microsoft BI, Grow, or Tableau.

Finally, the results cannot be kept just to the implementation team. They must be shared with everyone in order to create transparency and organizational-wide learning.

Step 6
SUMMARY AND REFLECTIONS

SUMMARY

If you think you have communicated your message enough, say it at least three more times across different channels, if possible; maybe then the stakeholders will start to pay attention. No matter how hard you try, you cannot over-communicate change. Change management takes a tremendous amount of organizational effort and should never be underestimated. According to a recent *Forbes* article, 70% of organizational change efforts fail. The reasons cited are many, such as a weak culture or one that is not aligned with the change mission, a lack of participation and buy-in, and of course lack-of or poor communication, training, and ongoing resources.

Moreover, you need to be honest with yourself about what has happened in the past within the organization regarding change. As stated in a *Forbes* article "When change efforts have failed in the past, people often grow cynical. They start to mutter under their breath, 'Here we go again...' or

'Here comes another flavor of the month…' or, as one middle manager once told me, 'We're lying low until this fad blows over.'"

I would suggest this is a typical sentiment for many organizations, so be honest with yourself and recognize the effort this change is really going to take. If you are going to transform your customer experience, your entire organization will need to be committed.

REFLECTIONS

- Have there been change initiatives in the past that have failed? If so, why, and what will be needed to ensure that your CX initiative does not follow the same pattern?

- Are you prepared to make a strong case? The best *why* is unassailable data that proves ROI.

- What internal channels do you have to communicate the CX initiative? What channels could you create that would resonate with staff?

- Who will be your CX champions? Make a list: they will be the core of your team.

Step 7
MEASURE THE RESULTS, AND ITERATE

AS DISCUSSED IN Step 3, the pace of organizational improvement is determined by the pulse of measured results against set goals. If you review and analyze your customer journey metrics twice a year, you can expect real improvement to happen twice per year. To begin, your implementation team should meet weekly to analyze results and the roll out of the implementation plan. Once your customer experience transformation is established, marry your customer journey reviews to an existing process, such as a monthly managers' meeting. Adding this report to an already-standing meeting will allow for easier ongoing adoption.

Inherently, each metric will provide an action item. For instance, if the conversion rate is below the goal, then the action item is to determine why and create a change to move the conversion rate up. This general tactic can be used for each of the eight KPIs, keeping in mind that there are more intricacies for some KPIs than others.

Real on the court implementation of new processes is hard

and messy. When an organization has been acting one way for years and now a new way is being preached and measured there will be a lot of resistance.

This is where objective metrics matter. If you use the outcomes as learning points as opposed to punitive measurement for corrective action, your chance of getting support and buy in for improvement tactics will obviously be much higher.

Let's review a sample scenario.

As the project lead for a new customer experience initiative, Jennifer has been excited for weeks. She has been assigned to lead a team to design a new customer journey with the goal to increase the NPS score by 10 and reduce the customer churn by 20% over the next year. For these two metrics she decided to measure the NPS monthly and churn every quarter. When she reviewed the current customer journey map she noticed the after sale and retention and referral stages do not have many touchpoints in her organization. Essentially, after the delivery of the product, the customer does not receive any further contact other than an NPS survey (of which completion percentages are quite low) and acquisition marketing messaging, unless there is a warranty concern. After the sale her organization is hands off the customer, leaving the customer to decide the next action if one at all.

She decides to implement two main new additions to the current customer journey. The first is to add a statement at the end of the purchase, in which the customer receives a survey within a week. The second is to implement nurturing marketing campaigns to existing customers, showcasing additional products to purchase that generally accompany the last purchase the customer made.

With these two changes made, it is now time to measure and iterate.

The first month results came back and the NPS actually went down. The change in the sales process informed customers that a survey was coming and as a result the email in their inbox was deleted less and responded to more. The increase in response rate increased the amount of passive responses, which ultimately drove down the NPS. Obviously, just getting an increase in survey response did not improve the NPS, the core issue of a mediocre score had been left untouched. During the next month, the subsequent iteration gave them time to review the NPS surveys for pain points and they chose one to tackle.

By the end of the initiative's first quarter, the retention rate had improved and the nurturing campaign was bringing back more customers—if only slightly more—as a 1% increase in retention was recorded. With this immaterial result, there was time to iterate and make a change to the current journey maps.

As you can tell, change is hard and messy and the path is not always clear. The key is to have a process in which these data points are reviewed regularly, followed up with an action plan for creation of the next iteration. This process ensures continuous improvement is occurring and that your organization is constantly working on its customer journey.

BEST PRACTICE

DECIDING WHERE TO FOCUS FIRST

When you review the eight KPIs and are trying to decide where to put your time and effort, there are several points to consider.

First, focus on what can be done quickly with very little cost. These changes, by definition, are fast and cheap and do not have a lot of barriers. A quick tweak to several key touchpoints (or moments of truth) can add up to the same effect as one larger, more expensive, and time-intensive tweak. The benefit of going after this low-hanging fruit is that the quick wins build momentum and resolve for the organization to then go after larger, longer-term changes. For instance, focusing on increasing the close rate can be a relatively quick change that will have a big impact to revenue immediately, while increasing the NPS takes longer to achieve and longer yet to see increased revenue results.

When making changes, focus on one touchpoint at a time in order to improve. Create the change, monitor/measure, learn and iterate for more improvement and then move to the next step. The hardest part is often choosing where to focus. To help with selection of touchpoints a simple graphing exercise will help.

Plot the various touchpoints you are considering for improvement along a vertical axis of greatest impact to the company and a horizontal axis of greatest impact to the customer. The outcome of this exercise will highlight the value impact for each touchpoint. To select you just simply cross reference with time and cost; answering the question: by changing a touchpoint which one will bring the greatest impact to the company and customer for the least amount of cost?

After all the quick wins are accomplished and the increases are solidified, go after increasing the data point that you feel will radically transform your business. For instance, if your customer churn is 80%, what would your business have to do to have a churn as low as 40%, and what would it look like for your organization to get there? More than likely, you would have to radically transform your approach to your customers. This now becomes the key metric in your business strategy moving forward.

Once you have determined the metric that will radically transform your business, you still may be stuck as there are many different touchpoints or moments of truth that influence the key metric. Go back to the plot graphing exercise described above, to prioritise the touchpoints to tackle.

Step 7
SUMMARY AND REFLECTIONS

SUMMARY

CREATE A SCHEDULE of review that is consistent, at a frequency that establishes your pace of change. Your reviews will be focused on measuring results against your goals and brainstorming iterations to create ongoing improvement. Note at times that setbacks will occur. Embrace the learnings from these setbacks to understand what doesn't work as opposed to becoming discouraged.

REFLECTIONS

- What current meeting schedule could your customer journey metrics review be included on?

- When you encounter poor results, are you willing to authentically seek the causes? Objective measurement cannot be dismissed. Improvement will at times require uncomfortable changes.

Step 8
COMMUNICATE THE RESULTS:
CREATE A DATA DEMOCRACY

IF YOU HAVE goals that you measure, your best chance of success is to have a data democracy around these goals. WhatIs.com defines a data democracy as a reference and self-education tool related to information technology; it is the ability for information in a digital format to be accessible to the average end user. The goal of data democratization is to allow non-specialists to be able to gather and analyze data without requiring outside help.

Thus, your customer journey data needs to be transparent and shared widely. To aid this, implement data visualization dashboard software. Spend the time to learn the platform that works best for your organization.

Placing all your results in a dashboard for all to see will cause several outcomes:

- The more data you share for all to access, the more insights on results you will receive. Moreover, the goals become everyone's goals as opposed to just management's goals.

- By sharing results, the transparency can create accountability, if this data democracy is used with the proper intent. With results available for all to see, all the good experiences and the poor experiences are showcased or exposed, and when it comes to your customer's experience as a result of organizational efforts, there should be nothing to hide.

- A regular review of the results: When used with the intent to learn, as opposed to being corrective, can create a learning culture that is hungry for the next dashboard iteration as opposed to dreading the newest results.

The timing of publishing results will dictate the learning pulse of your organization.

Obviously, the closer to real time you can publish results, the better. If your team can see what happened yesterday, they have an opportunity to get better today. If the reporting data cycle is monthly, the improvement iterations will be 12 times a year as opposed to daily.

The faster your reporting pulse, the more frequently you will improve: think monthly (12 times) versus weekly (52 times) or daily (250 times). Having a weekly pulse as opposed to a monthly pulse could equal a four-fold improvement versus monthly. When you start reporting on your data keep in mind the time it takes to produce reports. Ideally, all metrics are measured and the dashboards are automated. Most likely, that will not be the case, at least at the start. Be mindful of this, as well as your organization's capacity to enact change. There is nothing more disheartening than knowing what needs to be done and continually not being able to execute due to a lack of resources or unrealistic expectations. For these reasons, I often choose a weekly reporting cadence. Whatever your reporting pulse, the dashboard needs to be reviewed and analyzed with documented actionable insights for improvement to occur. Without an effective review process, the dashboard becomes just a bunch of numbers and graphs that do not make any difference at all.

The last piece of the puzzle must be education about what the data is telling the end user. You are fluent with the eight KPIs that can transform your business; however, if you implemented this system today, what percentage of your staff would understand the data? Ongoing training and support describing what the KPIs mean and what the organizational goals are in relation to the published KPIs will provide context. Just as publishing results and not taking action on those results make the dashboards redundant, so too does lack of understanding. As you seek to understand your customer experience through data, be sure to train your team so they can understand alongside you.

Sample Dashboards

KPI #1 - Total Advertising Reach

Reach is a measurement of the total number of potential and current customers or clients who are exposed to your offering in a given time period.

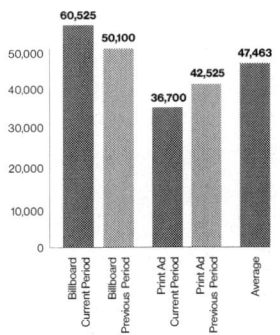

KPI #2 - Conversion Rate

Conversion rate is a simple ratio determined by the number of leads obtained divided by the reach of a channel.

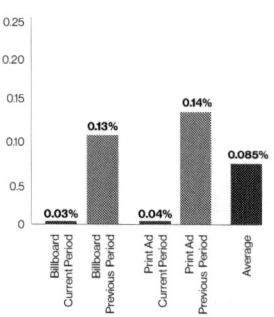

KPI #3 - Lead Count

The purpose of marketing is to create opportunity; for most organizations, opportunity equals leads.

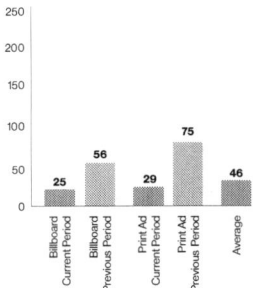

Step 8
SUMMARY AND REFLECTIONS

SUMMARY

Data democracy is the future of organizations. Embrace the cultural shift or be left behind. Employees expect to know what is going on and to be able to learn how to improve; the challenge for many organizations is in embracing and supporting this shift. Embracing this customer-centric shift and reporting on these metrics aligns with another macro shift occurring in organizations today: digital transformation. Quite simply, organizations are working to digitize their processes to better serve their customers. Digital processes are faster, consistent, and on-demand. As you work through this framework, the need to create reports will help in determining the processes to digitize first, as anything digital can be measured, reported upon, iterated, and subsequently improved.

After accuracy, consistency is required for continuous improvement to occur. Whatever reporting cadence is adopted, do not waiver from it, as that will present the

initiative as being unimportant and/or will cause teams to stop working on improvement, only to be jolted back into a start once an inconsistent process randomly occurs.

REFLECTIONS

- How much data is currently shared in your organization? Make a list.

- Do you use dashboards or other methods for creating accountability and insights? If so, can they be leveraged for your CX initiative?

BRINGING IT ALL TOGETHER: KICKING OFF YOUR CUSTOMER EXPERIENCE STRATEGY

"Nobody said it was going to be easy, and nobody was right!"

-George H.W. Bush

REBECCA, A CUSTOMER service manager for a small retail chain of four stores, stared at an email from an irate customer—a lost customer. Yet again, no one had gotten back to the customer when they requested information. Or at least not in the way in which the customer wanted to receive the information. This customer had sent an email, and sales had replied to the email with a phone number which the customer could call during business hours. When questioned, sales pushed back, indicating that in order for them to capture the lead they wanted the customer to call, and if the customer wouldn't call they were not that serious anyway.

Rebecca rubbed her eyes in frustration. In this case, the lost customer worked in a job in which they couldn't call during business hours and simply wanted to gather information to start the buying process. So, according to the customer email, "Due to the fact that your staff couldn't be bothered to fill a simple request, I am going to take my business elsewhere." These emails were becoming all too common, but no one seemed to care enough to do anything about it other than complain. More worryingly, no one seemed to know how many customers were being lost. Until recently, these emails were only just starting to be centrally captured; while that was progress, it did not answer the ultimate question that was racing through Rebecca's mind: *Just how bad is our customer experience?*

With that thought spurring action, Rebecca started to formulate a plan to change the customer experience at her company. She knew she would need to convince the top leadership that a change was necessary and that this wasn't just another fad management training initiative. To do that, she would need some facts. The owner had always stressed to get the facts before judgement is passed and/or decisions are made.

But what facts could she get without a budget to gather data? What did the company already have or could acquire at a minimal cost to implement? She knew she would need to talk to three groups to learn what was available. She looked up the controller, the IT manager, and the marketing manager.

From accounting, Rebecca expected to easily obtain: Average Transaction Size and Customer Churn by reviewing reoccurring revenue.

She felt IT would be able to provide a list of customers with emails. Armed with that list moving forward, she could conduct NPS surveys consistently for very little cost.

Marketing could then provide insights into the start of the buyer's journey. What is the total reach per month, plus were the marketing campaigns acquisition, retention, or reactivation oriented? In addition, the conversion rate for many of the channels should be tracked.

Starting with finance, what Rebecca discovered was shocking. Customer churn was a high 70%, and of the customers obtained when surveyed (with emails obtained from IT) the NPS was a low 32; moreover, when the NPS surveys were segmented between repeat customers and new customers, the NPS told a far different story. Existing repeat customers provided a reasonable NPS of 47, while new customers were at 17. Further, 50% of the respondents in the first surveys were existing customers skewing the results. The reality was, factoring in the 70% churn rate, a weighted average NPS of 26 was not very good at all.

From marketing, Rebecca learned that the overall conversion rate was 2.5% (which, having not benchmarked this, she could not evaluate); she also learned that marketing acquired leads and then handed them off to sales when deemed qualified. These leads then fell out of the sales funnel dramatically. This correlated to the email complaints she received from customers who felt the organization had not responded to their email requests appropriately. To this point, marketing provided the following insightful statistics about the business: In any given time period t, 20% of marketing acquired leads actually closed and became customers, but of the remaining 80% that did not purchase, 45% indicated they had not purchased because no one had gotten back to them in a timely or appropriate manner. So, in effect, if 100 leads came during time period t, 20 became sales and 36 did not receive an experience that enticed them to continue their journey. Considering a close rate of 20%, the organization was losing seven customers per time period for a lack of creating a positive customer experience. Considering the average transaction size was $2,500, the organization was losing $17,500 in revenue per time period t.

Lastly, marketing admitted that there was no specific retention marketing to current customers other than the general company sales email that went to all customers (either existing or potential) monthly.

Rebecca now had enough data to prove there was a problem. She needed to compile this data and convince the executive team to make changes.

To start, her strategy focused in two areas. Lead Management and Customer Retention. Her pitch to the executive team was simple. By closing more of the incoming leads, we already receive and retaining more of the customers we already have acquired, revenues can be increased dramatically. She proposed that the close rate could be increased by 7% (which was merely 20% of the mishandled incoming leads) and the retention rate by 5%. These two tactics combined would increase sales by 12%, considering that the returning customers average transaction size was the same as the overall average transaction size.

Starting her pitch with the headline **"Improving our customer's journey will increase sales by 12%,"** she had the executive team sitting up and listening. Now they wanted to know how this was going to be done, by whom, and by when.

Rebecca outlined her plan. First, a cross-functional team would need to be gathered. She requested representatives from marketing, sales, operations, and finance. Second, the organization needed to objectively know what its customers were experiencing. Rebecca argued that in order to know where to improve, the current customer journey needed to be understood and mapped. In addition, data on touchpoints would need to be gathered so that further understanding could be gleaned. That said, to obtain the 12% increase, two areas would be focused on first: incoming lead management and after sales experience.

With the journey mapped and regular data being gathered and reviewed, the outcomes would be measured for progress against the two stated goals of this program—increase the close rate by 7% and increase the retention rate by 5%.

Rebecca then elaborated that to further understand the customers, detailed target market profiles for each customer segment would be created, and armed with all this knowledge only then would the customer journeys be redesigned. Rebecca felt that to start an entire revamp of their customer journey was not needed, but an addition at the end (due to the absence of customer retention marketing) and rerouting of some of the beginning was required.

To ensure success, Rebecca stated that top-down buy in would be essential. As such, she requested a letter from the President to all staff about this initiative, and then a series of town hall meetings at each location to outline the current situation and the future direction. This would be followed up by quarterly updates to all staff of progress, training on new processes, and goal dashboards accessible to the team members involved. Rebecca felt that this new culture would take a year at least to "bake in" and become a way of being for the organization. With that stated, she was quick to point out that improving the customer experience never stops. This is not a short project we are launching; this is an ongoing process. The executives nodded their understanding.

Rebeca then laid out the best news to the executive team: other than some travel costs and minor software costs, this initiative needed no new funding. The focus was on priority, time, discipline, customer understanding, and support to start to see changes.

The executive team agreed. Now Rebecca had to assemble a team and bring the vision of an enhanced customer experience for her organization to life. The easy part of showcasing the problem and the reverse opportunity was done; now the real work would begin.

THE FUTURE OF THE CUSTOMER EXPERIENCE: BE GREAT OR BE GONE

THE FUTURE IS now, today. Customer expectations are increasing at an exponential rate. Waiting until the next quarter or next year to act is too late.

An IBM Institute for Business Value report brings this fact into sharp focus:

- **76% of consumers expect organizations to understand their individual needs.**

- **81% of consumers demand improved response time.**

- **68% anticipate organizations will harmonize consumer experiences.**

Currently, a gap is being created between what customers expect and what companies are delivering. Consider the following quote: "Merely meeting expectations is a myth. No one 'meets expectations' you either exceed expectations or you fall short."

What do the future expectations of customers look like, and thus what is the vision required for future customer journeys?

The future state is very hard to predict, but most experts point to expectation in the near future. Customers will expect the following as basic standards for all leading brands:

1. **Seamless experience**: Customers today expect that an interaction with a brand via one device or agent will be picked up right where they left off by another device or agent. The challenge brands have today is connecting all their management information systems to work together and capturing the required data so that this can occur. In the future, the lack of a seamless experience will not be accepted, as customers will not tolerate the inconvenience.

2. **360 degree understanding of the customer:** With more and more data being provided by customers, they expect something in return. Customers expect that the brands know their needs, situation, and desires (this is being amplified by e-commerce recommendation engines and social media interest algorithms). The transfer of that digital reality to physical brand experiences is not a far leap, and is already occurring. As a lack of a seamless experience will be considered an inconvenience and not tolerated, so too a lack of customer understanding will produce a negative customer purchasing behavior. Depending on the industry, it will manifest itself in several ways. In the service industry, customer

loyalty will continue to erode if a brand does not understand the individual; customers will default to brands that "know" them and make the service experience more tailored to their desires. In retail, there will be missed revenue opportunities. In B2B, customers will expect understanding as part of supply chain partnerships and a lack of understanding by the brand may affect the ability of the customer to meet their result targets, which will then put the supplier relationship at risk.

3. **Anticipation of needs**: The next stage of customer understanding is knowing what the customer may need or want before they do. This will become a method of retention for brands. Again, e-commerce is the obvious example in the current environment, with the suggestions of what other customers that purchased an item X also bought; if you are buying downhill skis you most likely need boots and poles. Further to this, brands are using social listening to help customers. A great example is when an individual posts a question on a social platform and the brand responds with a helpful answer that may or may not involve use of a brand's product or service. This basic B2C example gets more in depth with B2B integrated supply chain management, in which vendors are monitoring data from customers and receiving alerts to help mitigate potential issues. Machine learning is dramatically helping reduce the subject matter expert requirements in this area, thus allowing brands to automate this process.

4. **An expectation to receive unexpected (delightful) interactions:** What have you done to delight me lately? The final iteration of customer understanding and anticipation of needs is creating experiences that are unexpected but fit with the customer profile. Current manifestations of this are when brands allow customers to customize their own interface with supplier online portals or website homepages, so the customers receive only what they want to receive. Once this individualization is done and the data from multiple customers is combined and analyzed, unexpected suggestions can be made based on what other customers are doing or what is foreseen to make an experience with the brand or product more effective for them. Physically, this can occur by knowing your customers so intimately that you are able to surprise and delight them by anticipating their needs and requirements. The use of artificial intelligence to make suggestions will be critical to creating these unexpected customer experiences, at scale.

To actualize this future, companies will need appropriate customer data within integrated systems, which will then apply artificial intelligence and machine learning to achieve this future. These four elements will enable better predictions and enhanced service that can be automated 24/7 to meet customer needs, independent of human staff and interactions. According to a recent issue of the *Directors Journal*, a publication of the Institute of Corporate Directors, "Artificial Intelligence (AI) is going to influence almost every enterprise over the next five to ten years, and it will be the organizations that can best determine how to leverage the technology that will emerge as tomorrow's most competitive businesses." This is a prediction I agree with. This national institution is taking steps to educate its members on the topic so Canadian directors can ready their organizations for this shift.

In practical terms, what does this looks like?

In the good old days, an amazing customer-facing staff could make all the difference. Being friendly is free and it could go a long way; coupled with competency and fair pricing, that is all a brand needed to create a successful experience. Furthermore, if a brand could create scalable processes to train all staff to be friendly and competent, as long as the pricing remained competitive, the sky was the limit for an organization.

In today's world, people are still crucial, but being friendly is not only free, it is expected. Competency in relation to customer-facing staff's knowledge of products and service is no longer a differentiator between brands, it is now considered ubiquitous due the knowledge a smartphone can impart in 10 minutes or less. Competency is now measured as an overall organizational assessment. Competency for an organization is about how seamless the experience is for the customer, and how much or little of effort is required for the customer to do business with the organization. This means that your people must be armed with management information systems that instantly provides all the required information about the customer and the customer journey, so that the customer only needs to talk to one person to get what they need.

Your team must be connected by technology to the customer and to all your internal processes. In order to provide a seamless experience, organizations will need to have a 360-degree understanding of their customer. This will mean an individual measurement of each customer's individual journey with the brand and thus intimate knowledge of the customer must be available to all members of the team. With relationship selling, this means becoming a trusted advisor and capturing current and future customer needs in key account plans that can be accessed by all and executed by all.

Becoming a trusted advisor of a customer and capturing information about customer needs through consultative selling allows the next step, the anticipation of needs, to become possible.

It is important to note that while this book is a framework for improved customer journeys and thus customer experience, like the frame of house, you have to fill in the walls to complete it. As each house is different, each company is different, and each company can create its own differentiation in the marketplace using this framework to measure the improvement made upon its designed customer journey.

What works for one company may not work for another, a fact that Amazon CEO Jeff Bezos highlighted in a recent letter to shareholders: "We never claim that our approach is the right one—just that it's ours—and over the last two decades, we've collected a large group of like-minded people. Folks who find our approach energizing and meaningful."

My challenge to you is to figure out what works for your customers and your organization. Find your approach to your customer journey using the framework in this book to guide you. You can begin to meet this challenge just by starting. Start enhancing your customer's journey today. You and your customers will not be disappointed that you took that first step.

FORMULAS/DEFINITIONS

Average Revenue Per Account (ARPR): This is a key metric for subscription-based organizations but is also a key metric for organizations with key accounts, using strategic account management. The directional movement of this number is an indicator of the health of the customer base an organization has. The ARPR is a simple calculation. **ARPR = Total revenue of accounts/# of accounts.** To determine trends, simply compare ARPR relative to time period. Quarterly comparisons are typical, though shorter time periods may be needed.

Average Transaction Size: The average transaction size is a key measurement for understanding your business. It is needed to calculate the ROI or the projected ROI. The average transaction size is the average sale of a specific cohort in a specific time period. That could be a product grouping, location, department, customers or individual salesperson. Each of the cohorts can be analyzed for various reasons. For instance, tracking the average transaction size over time or location may be indicative of saturation or lack of saturation of customer accounts (sell more or less over time to

your customers). The calculation is conducted as follows:
ATS = Total Cohort revenue in time period t/number of transactions.

<u>Example:</u> Sales for the month of June by Sales Person X = $104,500/10 (10 transactions in the month of June. ATS = $104,500/10 = $10,450

BPM: Business Process Management: Business process management is a discipline in operations management in which people use various methods to discover, model, analyze, measure, improve, optimize, and automate business processes. BPM focuses on improving corporate performance by managing business processes. Any combination of methods used to manage a company's business processes is BPM. Processes can be structured and repeatable or unstructured and variable.

Churn Rate: Churn rate, or the opposite calculation of retention rate, refers to the number of customers that do not repeat purchases with an organization during time period t. To calculate the churn rate, first calculate the retention rate. The retention rate is calculated by taking the number of returning customers and dividing that by the total customers over time period t and converting this number to a percentage. The Churn Rate is then calculated by the difference of retention rate from 100%.

<u>Example:</u>

Consider time period t = one year
Total customers = 1000
Returning customers = 100

Retention Rate = 100/1000 × 100 = 10%
Churn Rate = 100% – retention rate
Churn Rate = 100% – 10% = 90%

Click Through Rate (CTR): The click through rate is the conversion rate of an online ad. Increase the CTR and you will have an opportunity to increase your leads. Generally, a click does not equal a lead. That is why the CTR combined with the conversion rate of your web property have become important data points for understanding your business's conversion rate for creating opportunity (leads).

Close Rate: The percentage of leads that become billable sales invoices over a measured time period. **Close rate % = # of sales/leads**

Example: For time period t: 10 sales/100 leads × 100 = Close Rate of 10%

Conversion Rate: The percentage of impressions that convert into a lead. This is often a metric managed for PPC (Pay Per Click) search terms or display ads. This is not to be confused with the Click Through Rate (CTR), which is another common metric used for online advertising. What a marketer is after is the rate at which an ad or activity converts at. To put this in mathematical terms consider the following: **CR = Leads/Impressions × 100**

Example: CR = 10 (Leads)/1000 impressions × 100 = 1%.

The goal of the marketer is to understand how to meet the needs of the customer in their messaging in order to increase the conversion rate. The higher the conversion rate, the higher the number of leads obtained.

Cost Per Click (CPC): A typical digital marketing calculation taking the total direct cost of the digital spend divided by the number of clicks achieved in the measured time period. **CPC = (ad spend + direct costs)/clicks.**

Example: If ad spend + direct costs = \$500 and there were 37 clicks over time period t, CPC = \$500/37 = \$13.5 per click.

This metric is used as a leading metric to help marketers understand performance of ad sets and/or digital platforms. Impressions are an aggregate metric of a channel, CPC is a measurement of traffic to an online property be that a website, landing page, or microsite. Analyses comparing the volume of clicks and CPC become important for evaluating various ad sets within a channel and/or advertising channels in of themselves. By itself, it is a comparative metric. When combined with a lead generation conversion rate, it is useful for understanding the total costs required to acquire a customer.

Cost Per Impression (CPI): Cost per impression is a marketing metric used to measure the cost per impression received, and is helpful with evaluation of channels. If the cost per impression is higher or lower than other channels, a marketer wants to know why. The aggregate cost of \$5,000/month for channel A versus \$6,500/month for channel B is meaningless without the comparison CPI. **CPI = the Total Impressions/Total Channel Cost in time period t.**

Example: CPI = \$5,600/10,000 = \$0.56 per impression.

Cost Per Lead (CPL): The cost to acquire a lead through advertising and promotional efforts. A typical calculation will be by channel. **CPL = Total Channel Cost/# of leads in time period t.**

Example: A print ad was run for $5,000, a total direct cost that resulted in 50 leads. CPL = $5000/50 = $100/per lead.

This is a very helpful metric for evaluating channels and internal training. If your sales team knows that each lead costs $100.00 they may be more motivated to optimize every opportunity that is presented.

CRM: Customer Relationship Management Software is a category of software that covers a broad set of applications designed to help businesses manage many of the following business processes: customer data, customer interactions, access to customer information, automate and optimize the sale process, and track and manage leads.

Customer Acquisition Cost (AC): This equals the total direct costs for acquiring a new customer. With direct advertising, this is relatively an easy cost to determine if all lead sources are tracked when a new customer is acquired. Even if all new customer lead sources are not tracked, if leads per channel are tracked and the company close rate is known, then this metric can be calculated.

Total costs include: ad cost, production costs, labour costs to produce ad.

If all new customer lead sources are tracked, simply use the number of customers by source. If not, use lead tracking to determine total leads by source and use your organization's close rate to determine total number of new customers. **New Customers = total leads by source × close rate.**

Example:

NC = 100 × 20% = 20 new customers.

Over time period t: **AC = TC/# of customers acquired with channel** = 6750/20 = \$337.50 AC per customer.

This metric is helpful when comparing channels. If you have a low AC on one channel you will want to saturate that channel as much as possible before adding a more expensive channel. In addition, the total cost of the channel may not be as important if the number of leads is high, and thus has a lower AC.

Customer Effort: Customer effort is a broad term used to define how much effort a customer has to expend in order to complete a transaction with an organization. As a result of organizations reviewing customer effort, CES (Customer Effort Scores) has evolved. Typically, an organization will measure specific touchpoints in a customer journey such as booking a rental online. The CES survey would ask on a scale of 1–5, with 5 being the highest, how hard did you find booking a rental unit on our website? The theory is that the higher the score, the lower the customer experience, and then of course, the lower the retention rate, NPS, etc. A high CES is not a good number to have.

Customer lifetime value (CLTV): In marketing, the customer lifetime value is a prediction of the net profit attributed to the entire future relationship with a customer. The prediction model can have varying levels of sophistication and accuracy, ranging from a crude heuristic to the use of complex predictive analytics techniques.

ERP: Enterprise Resource Planning Software is an integrated system used by organizations to combine, organize, and maintain the data necessary for operations. Enterprise resource planning (ERP) is the integrated management of core business processes, often in real-time and mediated by software and technology. ERP is usually referred to as a category of business-management software—typically a suite of integrated applications—that an organization can use to collect, store, manage, and interpret data from these many business activities.

Gross Margin Contribution (GMC): The profit per transaction after reduction of direct selling costs. Selling costs could include Cost of Goods Sold (COGS); commissions, brokerage fees, and direct product advertising fees.

Formula: **GMC = Selling Price – Direct Selling Costs.**

This number is needed in order to conduct effective ROI calculations on marketing and selling campaigns.

Lead: There is plenty of discourse around what a lead is or is not. For the sake of this book, a lead is any individual that expresses a desire for your services/products that has the current or future ability to pay for said product/services. Most sales teams do not use this broad definition; they only focus on individuals that showcase immediate buying signals. This narrow focus dismisses a large percentage of customers that are still in the evaluation/consideration phase of buying. With a broad focus, an organization can begin to understand their total opportunity, not just their immediate opportunity.

Marketing Automation Software: A subset of customer relationship management (CRM) that focuses on the definition, segmentation, scheduling, and tracking of marketing campaigns. The use of marketing automation makes processes that would otherwise have been performed manually much more efficient, and makes new processes possible. Marketing automation can be defined as a process where technology is used to automate several repetitive tasks that are undertaken on a regular basis in a marketing campaign. Marketing automation platforms allow marketers to automate and simplify client communications by managing complex omni-channel marketing strategies from a single tool. Marketing automation assists greatly in areas such as lead generation, segmentation, lead nurturing, lead scoring, relationship marketing, cross-selling, upselling, retention, and marketing ROI measurement.

Marketing Return on Investment (ROI): At the end of all the advertising analyses, the ROI is the benchmark by which all channels and activities are measured. If the ROI is below the organization's threshold, it is an immediate flag for evaluation.

ROI = (Total Gross Margin Contribution – Total Direct Costs)/Total Direct Costs × 100 = ROI percentage

Example: If your Total Gross Margin Contribution from

running a promotion was $10,000 and the Total direct costs were $2,750 the ROI would be (10,000 − 2750)/2750 × 100 = 263% ROI.

Net Promoter Score (NPS): The Net Promoter Score asks the simple question on a scale of 1–10, with 10 being the highest, how likely are you to recommend the product or service. The score is then calculated by subtracting the percentage of promoters (those that answered 9 or 10) from the percentage of detractors (those that scored 6 or less).

Example: **NPS = Promoters (75%)—Detractors (25%) = 50.**

Tech Stack: A term used to describe the combined software solutions organizations are using to manage the entire scope of their operations. The modern movement is toward an integrated, cloud-based tech stack that allows all data from various systems to be shared and utilized for more in-depth business intelligence reporting. A typical example would be a tech stack consisting of marketing automation software, a CRM (customer relationship management), an ERP (enterprise resource planning) all providing data into business intelligence dashboards about one customer's interaction with the organization. This can include call history, website browsing history, quotes provided, customer data such as business size, numbers of employees, and transactions with the organization. A BI dashboard with access to this data may wish to report on customers from a certain location that have done X in revenues with the organization in order to know the top customers in an area. Alternately, customers with outstanding quotes and X number of touchpoints could be listed in an area for highly engaged prospect lists that a sales or marketing team engage.

UTM Codes: A UTM code is a simple code that you can attach to a custom URL in order to track a source, medium, and campaign name. This enables Google Analytics to tell you where searchers came from as well as what campaign directed them to you.

Voice of the Customer (VOC): A term used in business and Information Technology to describe the process of capturing customer's expectations, preferences, and aversions. Social listening tools and customer surveys aided by technology enables brands to understand customer wants/needs and rank them hierarchically.

WORKSHEETS/TEMPLATES

Advertising ROI: www.stevewhittington.com/roi-worksheet

Goal Worksheet: www.stevewhittington.com/goal-worksheet

Customer Journey Mapping Template: www.stevewhitting-ton.com/customer-journey-template

Target Market Profile Template: www.stevewhittington.com/target-market-profile-worksheet

INDEX

A

B

C

D

E

F

G

H

I

ACKNOWLEDGMENTS:

It takes a village to raise a child is an African proverb that implies an entire community of people must interact with children for children to experience and grow in a safe and healthy environment. The villages look out for the children, they support them and nudge them in the right direction from time to time when needed. Prior to embarking on writing a book I understood it to be a solo journey. For this, my first book it has turned out to be the opposite. The amount of support I have received to bring the vision of the customer journey framework to being, has been transformational.

To start, I need to thank my parents for instilling in me a love of reading. Writers read, albeit not all readers write. From this foundation of reading I knew that I wanted to write a book, although I did not know about what.

To that I must acknowledge Ted Rabski, in 2016 I began blogging about customer experience and the framework I developed for this book was first inked in a blog in July 2017. I shared the blog with Ted because I valued his opinion. His reply was less than I had hoped. He acknowledged that it was an interesting blog and that I made some good points, but in his words "So what? What are you going to do with this?"

That hanging question burned for almost a year until I decided I would write a small E-book that could be shared and downloaded. With that intent I took several weeks and pushed together some old blogs as an outline and "seed content" from the 50 plus presentations and speeches I had given on the topic since 2014, and started to form the structure. Then I realized I had something more than a mere 40-page e-book. I then needed help.

Reaching out to my network I was soon put in touch with Calvin Simpson, his team was there to guide and support me with the writing, design, production, and project management of the entire process. Without Calvin and his teams support (in particular my writing coach Alaina Leary) this book would not be what it is. Thank you Ernest Barbaric for this connection and ongoing support in the process.

I was overwhelmed by the response of my LinkedIn community when I solicited their opinion on book cover designs, thank you to all for voting in my survey and providing insightful feed back which influenced the end design.

I am very grateful to the reading group that supported me with the drafts, providing insights and encouragement through the process: Shannon Hewlko, Natasha Neacsu, and Nathan Ramsdale.

Through the entire process with all the support mentioned one individual stands out from the rest, Jennifer Thompson, prior to the book she had tirelessly edited my blogs and presentations. Most importantly during that process she challenged my thinking which has shaped my work. The book today is heavily influenced by her insights and edits and most importantly her nudges to dig deeper and reach a little higher while writing and explaining concepts.

I have been lucky in my peers, most certainly in the fellow member of the Flaman Group of Companies executive team, Dave Weightman, with whom I worked with for years on understanding and improving the customer journey at Flaman. I am also grateful to my agency partners Shayne and Julie Serediuk that have been optimizing the start of the customer journey for our clients as opposed to just advertising to customers. The interaction with these individuals and the teams that came together for implementation of customer journey improvements was the fertile ground in which my knowledge and skill set could grow. All the individuals involved contributed, thus the work of this book is their work as well.

Lastly, I must thank my wife for her support. Writing a book is a consuming task and for her part she was supportive of the entire process, that support at times was needed much more than I would have ever known.

72912195R00165

Made in the USA
Columbia, SC
02 September 2019